Sanity

☀ IN ☀ THE ☀

Summertime

The complete summer-survival
handbook for moms

D0711686

Other works by Linda Dillow:

Creative Counterpart
Priority Planner

Other works by Claudia Arp:

Almost 13
Ten Dates for Mates
60 One-Minute Marriage Builders
60 One-Minute Family Builders
60 One-Minute Memory Builders
Mom's Support Group Video Package
Mom's & Dad's Support Group Video Package

Sanity
✸ I N ✸ T H ✸ E ✸
Summertime

The complete summer-survival
handbook for moms

Linda Dillow and Claudia Arp

THOMAS NELSON PUBLISHERS
Nashville

Published in Nashville, Tennessee, by Thomas Nelson, Inc., and distributed in Canada by Lawson Falle, Ltd., Cambridge, Ontario.

Printed in the United States of America.

Unless otherwise indicated, Bible verses are taken from the New American Standard Bible, © The Lockman Foundation 1960, 1962, 1963, 1968, 1971, 1972, 1973, 1975, and are used by permission.

Verses marked KJV are from the King James Version.

Verses marked RSV are from the Revised Standard Version of the Bible, copyright 1946, 1952, © 1971, 1973.

Verses marked TLB are taken from *The Living Bible* (Wheaton, Ill.: Tyndale House Publishers, 1971) and are used by permission.

Library of Congress Cataloging-in-Publication Data

Dillow, Linda.
    Sanity in the summertime / Linda Dillow and Claudia Arp — Rev. and updated.
      p. cm.
    ISBN 0-8407-3188-4 (pb.)
      1. Child rearing—United States   2. Vacations—United States.
    3. Parent and child—United States.   4. Recreation—United States.
    5. Play. I. Arp, Claudia. II. Title.
    HQ772.D54   1991
    649'.5—dc20   90–44850
                                     CIP

1 2 3 4 5 — 94 93 92 91 90

To our wonderful children:
    Joy, Robin, Tommy, and Niki Dillow
    Jarrett, Joel, and Jonathan Arp

Contents

PREFACE   xi

CHAPTER 1
Oh, Super Mom, Where Are You?   13

CHAPTER 2
Making Summer Sane   16

CHAPTER 3
Children's Day   22

CHAPTER 4
"Just-Me-and-Mom" Time   46

CHAPTER 5
Communication Is Contagious   58

CHAPTER 6
Summer Strategies for Self-Esteem   69

CHAPTER 7
Plans for Producing   78

CHAPTER 8
Challenge Your Children   91

CHAPTER 9
Putting Sonshine in Your Summer   97

CHAPTER 10
Sharing Your Sonshine   109

CHAPTER 11
Traveling Made Triumphant   116

CHAPTER 12
    A Special Word to Wives . . . Husbands
       Have Summers Too   128

CHAPTER 13
    Summer Strategies for Mom   136

CHAPTER 14
    Walking the Two-Job Tightrope—Extra Helps
       for Working and/or Single Parents   145

CHAPTER 15
    Your Summer Plans   151

CHAPTER 16
    Disasters Turned to Delight   159

CHAPTER 17
    Be a Memory Maker   166

APPENDIX I   174

APPENDIX II   183

NOTES   187

INDEX OF CHILDREN'S DAY IDEAS   189

ABOUT THE AUTHORS   190

Thanks

To Helene Spencer for her creative artwork

To Jennifer Siler for her help in editing

Preface

When the first edition of *Sanity in the Summertime* was printed more than a decade ago, both the Dillow and Arp families were living in the heat of the battle for summertime sanity. Our children were our "guinea pigs" as we tested the ideas included in this book. Some were disasters, showing that we were not "Super Moms." Others were delights, indicating real hope. All in all, we were convinced that sanity in the summertime could be a reality for parents willing to pray, plan, and persevere!

Now as we are presenting to you an updated, revised edition of *Sanity in the Summertime,* we are looking at our summers from a different vantage point—that of the "empty nest." Yes, all seven sanity kids, including Niki, the Dillow's adopted Austrian son, have now left the nest, and two wonderful daughters-in-law have joined the Arp family.

Gone are the opportunities for us to plan one more summer, have one more Children's Day, give one more summer challenge and graduate one more kid into teenagehood! But still with us and our adult children are the wonderful memories of fun summers we shared together. Amazingly, we all tend to remember the positive things that happened, and even the few "disasters" that we remember can provoke laughter today.

Our own positive experiences and those of thousands of other parents who have used this book have convinced us more than ever, that the principles in this book work and are just as valid for the nineties as they were for the eighties. While our culture has changed greatly in the past ten years, the principles for building healthy relationships with our children remain the same.

Sanity in the Summertime was initially addressed to mothers, yet we know that many other people are care givers and influence our children. If you are a single parent, a dad, a grandparent, an aunt or uncle, a guardian, or a loving friend or neighbor, we hope you will find encouragement and practical helps within these pages to impress the children in your summers. For simplicity in writing, we still refer most often to mom, but our desired audience is all who love and influence children.

Another shift in our culture has been the change in the percentage of families in which both parents are employed outside of the home. If you fit into this category, we want to give hope and encouragement to you as well. Use this book to plan and benefit from the time you do have. To help you do this, we are including a special chapter for working and/or single parents. Planning the summer still works, even for parents with full-time jobs. The time factors won't be the same and the sanity level achieved might be a little lower, but spending time and nurturing your children is far more important in the long run than doing that extra hour of work one night a week. Also this book can be used by whoever keeps your children in the summer, perhaps even a neighbor. If there are saintly persons out there who keep kids during the summer—share this book with them!

Remember, the summers go by quickly. Before you know it, you will be joining the Arps and Dillows in the empty nest. Summer traditions, summer memories—ours for keeping, ours for treasuring, ours for sharing, ours for passing down to future generations.

Now is the time to begin. When you think about it, now is all the time you have—today, tomorrow, these coming three months. Now is the time for building for the future. Now is the time for sanity in the summertime!

CHAPTER 1

Oh, Super Mom, Where Are You?

Joan rested against the neighbor's fence as she shared the frustrations of getting the children off to school that morning. "Oversleeping was only the beginning," she confided to her friend Marg, "followed by no clean socks in the right color. Then I was the chief arbitrator as two apple lovers tried to make two lunches with one apple.

"As we were deciding who should take the apple, I heard Paul say to Kathy, 'One of us ought to act like a Christian about this—how about you!' With that, he grabbed the apple and made a beeline for the door."

Marg, who had no children, laughed, saying, "It does sound hectic, Joan, but think of the fun you have at your house!"

"Fun!" repeated Joan. "Just wait until you have children—you'll see. At least now I have some time to myself while the children are at school. But summer vacation begins in two weeks, and that is a new set of challenges."

Even as the words came out of her mouth, Joan began to see her family through the eyes of a woman who would gladly change places with her.

"I guess it is sort of fun," Joan admitted. "Maybe it's just that we don't realize it while it's happening. We're just too busy to enjoy our children."

God tells us that children are a heritage from Him. I'm sure we all agree, but as parents we know that children can be a *hectic heritage!*

One woman put it this way:

> I wished for home and husband;
> the wish was granted me . . .

My heart and hearth are daily sparked
with masculinity.

I wished for children.
This request was also granted me.
A nimble, five-ringed circus
Performing endlessly!

I'm ready for my third wish now
though squandered it may be . . .
A few dull moments . . .
Please, oh please, occasionally![1]

When June arrives, we know summer is upon us and the "nimble, five-ringed circus" is home to stay. Honestly, how do you look on these three months? Is it a time to build and mold your children? A time to build memories as a family? Or is it an interruption in your life, an inconvenience? Are you like the mother who confided, "I never would have made it through last summer without the child-care program. It was a real lifesaver!"

Four couples concocted a joint vacation plan one summer that worked so well that they planned to do it again. "Together we rented a country house for two months," explained one of the wives to a friend. "Each couple spent their two-week vacation there taking care of all thirteen of our collective children."

"You've got to be kidding!" exclaimed the friend. "I wouldn't call taking care of thirteen children a vacation!"

"Oh, the two weeks were a horrendous disaster," admitted the mother. "The *vacation* was the six weeks at home without the kids!"

"HAVE A COOKIE, HONEY"

Most of us don't go to such extremes to make our summers sane, but if you're like us you've probably done one or more of the following.

a. Separated yourself psychologically from the children at intervals during the day, muttering, "Mommy's busy. Go play now," or "Not now—can't you see I'm reading?" or "Have a cookie, Honey, and I'll be through in a minute." (This possibly explains the great amount of weight gained by children in the summertime.)

b. Checked off the days of summer and done a jig when Labor Day arrived.

    c. Had a "bad attitude" for eighty days and continually asked, "Why me, Lord?"

    d. Been the opposite of Proverbs 31:26: "She opens her mouth in wisdom, and the teaching of kindness is on her tongue." Need we describe the opposite?

OH, SUPER MOM, WHERE ARE YOU?

We've always heard that there are mothers who are naturally patient, loving, cheerful, never tired, and always smiling . . . mothers who awaken each day with a song, whose children never irritate them or bring them to tears . . . mothers who always know when and how to discipline, when and how to be creative with their children. They are Super Moms in every sense of the word. We've never met any, but we understand they exist.

We hope you are such a parent, but chances are you're more like us— not naturally patient, loving, or cheerful, often tired, and occasionally ready to pull your hair out! We weren't Super Moms; being the kind of mothers we wanted to be is the hardest thing we ever tried to do. But we grew and made progress, and our children say they wouldn't trade us even if they found someone better.

We wanted our summers not only to have sanity but also to be exciting, rich, and wonderful times with our children. We had several summers like that, and we are excited to be able to share with you some of the things we learned.

15

CHAPTER 2

Making Summer Sane

A farmer set out one morning to plow the "south forty." He left his house about five-thirty, figuring that he should get an early start because his tractor needed oil. After picking up the oil and walking a mile to the tractor out in the field, he discovered he had not brought enough oil. So he walked a mile back to the shop to get it.

On the way to the shop he noticed that the pigs had not been fed, so he proceeded to the corncrib, where he found some sacks of feed. These large sacks of feed resembled the sacks in which he stored his potatoes—and then he recalled that yesterday he had noticed his potatoes were sprouting. He immediately put down the sack of feed and headed toward the potato pit. As he passed the woodpile on the way to the pit, he remembered that his wife had asked him to get some wood for the stove if he wanted breakfast that morning. As he picked up a few pieces of wood, an ailing chicken passed by. He dropped the wood and began to tend to the chicken. Perhaps the rest of the chickens were similarly infected, he reasoned. So he called the veterinarian immediately.

When evening arrived, the frustrated farmer realized he never had finished putting oil in his tractor, nor had he plowed the field.[1]

Now if this fictional story seems a bit absurd, here's a true one. Recently a young mother of three got up late one morning (the alarm didn't go off). Actually, there was nothing wrong with the clock, but due to the turmoil of the evening before and the presence of late-night guests, she had forgotten to set the alarm. So the daily, frantic race to make the eight o'clock school bus was on. "Hurry up, kids! We're late!"

"I'm tired. I don't want to get up," murmured one child.

"I've got a sore throat," complained another.

"Oh, I forgot! We've got a test today, and I didn't bring my book home last night and I'll flunk!" shrieked the third.

Hurriedly, Mother rushed downstairs. While combing her hair she saw she had neglected to clean the downstairs bathroom, which the overnight guests would be using. *How embarrassing!* she thought. *What will they think of me as a hostess?* She ran back upstairs to the cabinet where the cleanser was kept—no cleanser! She had forgotten to put it on her shopping list.

Suddenly, a bloodcurdling scream erupted from the other room. "Nero ate my hat!" cried the middle child. "I hate that dog—dumb dog. Dumb, dumb, dumb!"

Finally, everyone was fed and ready to walk out the door with just enough time to make it to the bus. "Mommy, where is the money for the school pictures? I was supposed to have it yesterday, and if I don't have it today the teacher will get mad at me."

"Yeah, me too," the others joined in.

Mother opened her purse and found it empty. "Oh, I forgot. I was supposed to go to the bank yesterday afternoon. Do you kids have any money in your piggy banks?"

After she solemnly promised the children they would be repaid, they tore upstairs and opened their banks. Just enough!

Out the door they went to catch the bus, and finally a beautiful silence fell upon the house. Suddenly, three children burst through the door, crying, "We missed our bus!" So Mom drove them to school.

How many times do you find yourself in a similar situation? Instead of you controlling your circumstances, circumstances seem to control you. Like the farmer you start out to do something that you know is important, but you never seem to get it done. Or like the mother's your life is often in turmoil and chaos, seemingly beyond your control. And things seem worse in the summer when children are home.

MISSION: IMPOSSIBLE

Instead of drifting through June, July, and August, we decided to attempt "Mission: Impossible"—to turn summer from survival to sanity. In a word, we decided to *plan* our summer! Now we realize that planning is a horrible word—it reminds us of the many times we attempted to plan and failed.

One mother's recollection expresses well the regret of abandoning our plans.

Have you ever said, "I was going to, but there wasn't time?"

Time . . . what is it? Sixty seconds make a minute, minutes turn into hours, and hours into days. It zips by unnoticed or lingers forever when we're bored. What is it? Friend or foe? For the answer, take a moment to reflect on your past.

When I was a little girl, we were going to take a family camping trip; but my brother had a soccer game, Dad needed to work in the yard, and Mom didn't like bugs. Besides, there wasn't time.

When I was seven, we were going to read through the *Narnia* series as a family every Friday night, but Dad had to work late, Mom had to clean the kitchen, and our favorite TV program was on. There just wasn't time.

When I was nine, I got my first real bike, and we were going to take a bike hike as a family. But Mom's bike had a flat, my brother didn't want to go, and Daddy didn't have time.

When I was twelve and got my braces, Mom was going to take me out for a special lunch, and we were going to shop for my first bra. But company dropped in unexpectedly, the laundry needed doing . . . and there wasn't time.

When I grew up and left home for college, I was going to sit down with my parents and tell them how much I loved and appreciated them . . . and that I would miss them. But the last-minute packing took too long, I didn't want to miss my plane, and . . .

There just wasn't time.

What follows in this book is a step-by-step guideline for mapping out your summer with your children so it can be a time of rich enjoyment and maximum profit. Remember, we are only talking about the time from when school is out to when it begins—in our situation approximately eighty days. Too many times we think of planning for a lifetime or a year, and the odds are against our carrying through. After all, who could give up all fattening foods for the rest of their lives or run a mile a day for the next three years? But if we are talking about fewer than ninety days, the outlook for success is much brighter.

Psychologists tell us that it takes three weeks to feel comfortable with a new habit (or to break an old one), and six weeks to make it a part of your life. We are suggesting in this book that summertime sanity is not only surviving the summer but developing some new ways of relating to and enjoying your children—ways that, if practiced for the whole summer, will also benefit you when school starts again. We want you to reap the benefits much longer than the three months of summer!

MAKING SUMMER SANE

Let's say that you bought this book in September. The title probably attracted you because you have just had another horrendous summer and you wonder if somebody really does have some answers. You now have nine months, with the help of the suggestions in this book, to give birth to a plan that can turn your summer experience into real, enjoyable sanity!

On the other hand, if you bought this book in the spring, there is little doubt about what attracted you to it—not only a sense of failure, but one of fear and impending doom!

We found that three basic steps turned us around and put us on the road to summertime sanity. First, before taking any steps, we began praying about our summers. Then we asked ourselves these three questions:

1. *What* specific things do we want to see happen this summer?
2. *How* can we practically reach our objectives?
3. *When* will we carry out our plans?

In a closing chapter, we will go through each step, helping you put your plan in writing. But to get us started, let's set some objectives.

Objectives

For some of us it might seem quite unnatural to set objectives, but businesses thrive on goal-setting, and homes desperately need more of it. However, few parents set specific objectives for their family and personal development, much less draw up a plan to accomplish them. Why not use this summer to set some objectives for your family?

What is a summer objective? It is simply *what you want to accomplish* this summer. What would you like to see happen in your family? What would you like to see happen in your relationships with your children and your spouse? Writing these things down helps to focus your attention on making summer meaningful.

We decided to divide the objectives into three categories:

- Objectives related to our children (our main summer emphasis)
- Objectives related to our mates
- Objectives related to ourselves

Child-Related Objectives

Once we raised our "faith level" above the survival point, we were able to come up with six objectives in this category.

1. *To develop deeper personal relationships with your children.* How can you use this summer to get to know your children better? To spend time "together" without really spending time together is easy! How well do you really know your children? In the next two chapters we will be sharing information about Children's Day and "Just-Me-and-Mom" time—two ideas for developing a closer relationship with your children.

2. *To improve communication with your children and to help them express themselves better.* How can you help your "Timmy the Turtle" come out of his shell and become "talking Timmy"? How can you become a better listener and communicator with your children? We will share some practical tips and communication projects for you to try at your house this summer.

3. *To help your children develop better self-images.* How do your children view themselves? One key to children's self-esteem is their view of their parents' perception of them. And then how can you counterbalance the world's standard of beauty and brains? In our chapter on self-esteem we offer some suggestions for showing your children that "you're something special—you're the only one of your kind!"

4. *To help your children develop responsibility and competence.* One nice thing about summertime is that there is more unstructured time—unless you fill it up with twenty-five new activities! It provides many opportunities for you to help your children in areas that may go unnoticed during the hectic school year. However, this is one objective that will not "just happen" unless you plan and persevere. It would be wonderful if children would tackle responsibilities (whether chores or challenges) with as much enthusiasm as they tackle football. But in a popularity contest, chores would probably tie for last place with school work, brushing teeth, and going to bed. Our projects and suggestions will help you help your children develop responsibility and competence in new areas this summer.

5. *To encourage your children to grow spiritually.* What can you practically do this summer to strengthen spiritual growth in your children? How can you relate God to everyday situations? How can you teach your children to serve others? These and other questions will be discussed, along with projects and suggestions.

6. *To make travel time more enjoyable.* What can you do when

everyone is tired, cranky, hungry (and you've already gone through all the food), and you still have two hours to go? Planning tips will provide a touch of sanity to your summer travels.

Spouse-Related Objectives

To enrich your relationship with your mate. You need to remember that parents have summers, too. What can you do this summer to get to know your mate more intimately? In making your plans for the summer, you don't want to forget the one family member you had *before* you had your children. Face it: without *him/her* you wouldn't have a family—or eighty special days to plan for!

Personal Objectives

In the midst of all this planning to "give" to our families, what about "you?" The summer should also be a time in which you can grow as a person and not just tread water until September. In the chapter for moms we give several practical suggestions and projects to help you develop as a person this summer. Also included is a chapter of helps for single parents and those who work outside the home.

You've probably already heard, "Aim at nothing and you'll hit it every time!" On the other hand, when you plan and then don't achieve your desired goal, it's easy to get discouraged and give up. When September comes, you may not have completed *every* project and *every* activity you planned, but you will be much farther along the road to sanity than you were at summer's beginning.

We hope this September you won't have to look back on your summer and say, "There just wasn't time!"

CHAPTER 3

Children's Day

When is an ideal time to do creative, fun activities with your children?

To many it might seem to be . . .

> . . . when it's not raining and not too hot outside
> . . . when the laundry is all done and the house is neat and clean (Is it really possible to experience both at the same time?)
> . . . when dinner is in the slow cooker and the cookie jar is full
> . . . when there are no calls to return on your answering machine
> . . . when stacked-up letters are all answered and the phone is not ringing (or better still, it's out of order)
> . . . when no one has a runny nose, a dirty bottom, or an upset stomach
> . . . when you have had ten hours of sleep the night before and a nice, long oil bath
> . . . when your hair is washed and dried and your nails nicely manicured
> . . . when no one's favorite TV program is on and the neighborhood gang is ganging up at someone else's home

Surely the list could go on and on, and our conclusion would be that *no time is an ideal time to do fun things with our children!* But if your first objective is to develop closer relationships with your children, let us encourage you to begin by doing fun things together with them this summer.

"LET'S BUILD A SWIMMING POOL!"

To counteract all the negative odds at the beginning of each summer, we sat our dears down to come up with a list of things we could do together during the summer. Would you believe that both sets of children came up with the idea of building a swimming pool in the backyard? After we convinced them that this was *not* an option, they began to share other suggestions.

- go to the zoo
- camp
- visit an amusement park
- play tennis
- go on a train ride and a bus ride
- go to several different parks
- visit a museum
- play soccer
- have a party for no reason
- go bike riding
- go swimming every day
- go on lots of picnics

They got in the swing of it and continued to give suggestions all summer long! The surprising thing was that so many of their suggestions were easy to fulfill—and inexpensive.

"IT'S MY DAY, MOM!"

In June we initiated Children's Day. Our goal: *to do one special thing with the children each week.* Wednesday was the day set aside when mother and children would plan together how they would spend their day. One Wednesday was spent at the lake picnicking and swimming, another at the zoo, and another at home having a "Creative Craft Day." Sometimes we joined our two families for Children's Day, but often we went alone with our children. We found that when another mother was there, we mothers spent the day talking and the children "did their own thing" alone—lots of fun for us (we love "adult talk") but it destroyed our purpose of spending a day with our children.

Lest you think that every Wednesday was perfect, without flaw, let us assure you that such was not the case! There were Wednesdays when Children's Day just did not happen—when children were sick, when company came unexpectedly, when rain came on Picnic Day. But we can say with surety that because of planning Children's Day, we spent much more time than we would have doing fun things with the children—things they wanted to do!

23

The next step is to get your own creative juices flowing. The rest of this chapter contains suggestions to get you going. To cover a wider range of age groups we have made two basic divisions—one for school-age children and one for preschoolers. There probably will be some overlapping, especially if you have children in both age groups. And because we cannot control the weather, there is a further division of indoor and outdoor activities.

A WORD TO SINGLE PARENTS AND WORKING PARENTS

Before you just skip the section on Children's Day, let us encourage you to take a close look at what you can and cannot do. Probably you will not be able to take a day each week to spend uninterrupted time with your children, but you can use the time you have and maybe create some other opportunities as well.

Rather than Children's Day, you may have to set your sights on a regular Children's Hour. Or perhaps you can arrange your work so you can take off three days during the summer and plan three fantastic, super-special Children's Days. Each week, during children's hour, you could work and prepare for the special events like a backyard circus. One creative mother that we know takes off the fourth Tuesday morning of each month and calls it Children's Morning. The issue is not how much time you have, but how you are using the moments and minutes you do have. Planning special children's times into your summer will help them actually become reality. For more tips for working parents, see Chapter 14.

OLDER CHILDREN

With younger children your challenge as a mother in bringing off a successful Children's Day is mainly one of physical endurance. Once plans are set in motion, little ones tend to follow easily.

Not so with school-age children. Here the challenge is often one of emotional endurance and how to motivate them—how to make time with the family more appealing than peers, TV, and other competitors. One way to do this is to include them in the actual planning of Children's Day so it becomes their idea too. They also can be a help in the actual preparation. Here's a plan for Children's Day with school-age children.

Outdoor Fun

IDEA #1—POOL PICNIC (or lake, beach, river, mud hole, or whatever you can find!)

The afternoon before, let the children plan the picnic menu and, if possible, do the shopping. Remember to keep it simple. For example, favorite sandwiches, chips, fruit, and juice. Why not let the children make cookies the day before to take on the picnic? If you're super-organized, the cookies could be made the week before on a "Creative Cooking Children's Day" and frozen for the picnic. However, if time is short, you can buy cookie doughs that are ready for the oven. Then let the children decorate them with sprinkles, raisins, and candy.

On the big day, give each child an index card checklist of things to do before leaving.

```
_____ Get dressed
_____ Pick up room, including
          _____ bed neatly made
          _____ clothes in their proper place
                  (this means no clothes on floor, under bed, or crammed
                  behind the door!)
_____ Teeth brushed
_____ Assemble own activity bag
          _____ paper and pencil
          _____ book to read
          _____ ball, jump rope, etc.
          _____ games, cards
          _____ bug spray
_____ Help with picnic lunch (write in each child's responsibility)
```

You may be wondering who makes out the list—you do, Mom! But it's well worth the few minutes the night before to divide the chores and organize your helpers. It also cuts down on questions like "When can we go?" or fights among excited brothers and sisters.

Before you know it, you should all be enjoying the sun and surf (water and/or mud). Plan some good games like keep away or water basketball for slack times. Lunch can double as a good communication time with a few, well-thought-through questions or open-ended statements like "My favorite thing about swimming is . . ." or "The thing I like most about summertime is . . ." You could also play games or cards while waiting for your food to digest before you resume the water fun.

By three, you'll be heading home for cleanup, rest, and dinner. If you are quite clever you will have tanked up your slow cooker that morning, and you'll walk into the super aroma of:

BELIEVE IT OR NOT—CHICKEN IN THE POT
(4–6 servings)

1 3-pound chicken, whole or
   cut up
2 carrots, sliced
2 onions, sliced
2 celery stalks with leaves, cut
   in 1-inch pieces

2 tsp. salt
½ tsp. coarse black pepper
½ cup water or chicken broth
½ to 1 tsp. basil

Put carrots, onion, and celery in bottom of crock pot. Add whole chicken or chicken pieces. Top with salt, pepper, liquid. Sprinkle basil over top. Cover and cook on low setting until done (7 to 10 hours).

Serve with fresh fruit yogurt salad. (Cut your favorite fruits—or those you have on hand—into bite-size pieces and use your favorite fruit yogurt as dressing for a yummy salad.)

After dinner you're free to enjoy being with your mate or to curl up with a good book, knowing that for one day you qualify as "Super Parent!"

IDEA #2—A DAY AT THE MUSEUM

It's best to phone a week or two in advance and ask the museum director to mail you any printed information on the exhibits, museum distinctives, floor plan, and other helpful materials. The day's schedule might look like this:

   8:00 Rise and dress, picking up the rooms
   8:30 Light breakfast and devotions
   9:00 Everyone clean up the kitchen together
   9:30 Go over the museum brochures together, making sure
          everyone understands what they will be seeing and doing
10:15 Drive to the museum
11:00 Stop at a fast-food place for a hot dog or hamburger
11:45 Arrive at the museum and begin the tour

1:00 Milk break (remember—the kids' attention spans are not as long as yours)
1:15 Resume tour
2:30 Trip home
3:30 Rest, free time, and clean up for supper
6:00 Supper of previously prepared meal (perhaps the following slow cooker special)

SWISS STEAK
(4–6 servings)

2 pounds round or Swiss steak, cut ³/₄-inch thick
salt and pepper to taste

1 large onion, thinly sliced
1 can tomatoes (1 pound)

Cut round steak into serving pieces; season with salt and pepper, and place in slow cooker with sliced onion. Pour tomatoes over all. Cover and set on high for 1 hour and turn to low for 8 to 10 hours.

CREAMY SWISS STEAK

Follow recipe for Swiss Steak, substituting 1 can mushroom soup and ¹/₂ can water for tomatoes. Spread soup evenly over top.

Both of these recipes are delicious and take only minutes to prepare!

Indoor Fun—No Planning Needed

What do you do when a picnic and swim day is planned, but the day breaks rainy and cold and the children awaken disappointed and grumpy? You have two alternatives:

1. Tell the children, "Sorry, no Children's Day."
2. Claim 1 Thessalonians 5:18: "In everything [even rain] give thanks; for this is God's will for you in Christ Jesus."

To help you get started, here are three ideas of how to create an indoor Children's Day without going to the store and spending money. A good beginning for each of these three ideas is to make Aggression Cookies—guaranteed to relieve grumpiness and rainydayitis!

AGGRESSION COOKIES

Yield: 15 dozen (you might want to cut the recipe in half unless you want to feed an army!). Preheat oven to 350°.

Combine:

6 cups oatmeal	3 cups flour
3 cups brown sugar	1 tsp. baking soda
3 cups margarine	

Mash, knead, and squeeze "until you feel better" and until there are no lumps of margarine. Next, form the dough into small balls, not as big as a walnut, and put on an ungreased cookie sheet. Butter the bottom of a small glass and dip it into granulated sugar. This is used to flatten each ball of dough, dipping it into sugar each time.

Bake 10–12 minutes. Remove when lightly brown, cool a few minutes, and crisp on a rack. Store in a tight container. The dough keeps well in the refrigerator.

IDEA #1—CREATIVE COLLAGE

Materials needed:

1. Paper—construction paper is great but anything will do. We often used the back of computer paper.

2. Glue (glue sticks if you have them)

3. Variety of whatever can be found in "Mother Hubbard's Cupboard," as long as it's "glueable."

    a. egg noodles, spaghetti noodles, macaroni, etc.

    b. kidney beans, pinto beans, soy beans, etc.

    c. Cheerios, cornflakes, other cereal

    d. aluminum foil

    e. drinking straws

    f. toothpicks

    g. raisins, peanuts, marshmallows, etc.

How to create the collage:

1. Place all "glueable" items in center of table.

2. Give a supply of glue to each child (if you can only find one bottle, squeeze a small amount of glue into a paper cupcake holder or onto a piece of foil and let the child use a toothpick to apply the glue).

3. Give each child a piece of paper and let him/her create a

masterpiece—perhaps a house with flowers, an animal, or an "original" anything!

4. Display "masterpieces" and have an impromptu art show for family or friends.

    a. Serve Aggression Cookies

    b. Display art work

IDEA #2—SLIDE OR VIDEO SHOW

When rain has spoiled the picnic or the broken-down car makes the museum trip impossible, try a family slide show.

Materials needed:

1. Slides of family, perhaps of children from birth to present, summer vacations, friends, relatives, places you've lived, places you've visited, any family pictures

2. Paper, pen, crayons, or washable markers

3. Slide projector or video camera and tape

Activity:

1. Let the children go through the slides and pick out the ones they want. You can help with the selection (to insure that they don't choose any of you in your bathing suit!). If preparing a video, have children draw pictures of family members or special events they remember, or have them dress up in Mom and Dad's clothes and tell a funny story.

2. Together, arrange slides or pictures to tell a story of your family.

3. Write a script (the funnier the better) to go with the slides or pictures. Let the children do as much of the creative thinking and writing as possible.

4. Have a "sample" showing when all is organized.

5. Later that evening or another day, have a "real" showing for the family or perhaps the children's friends. Have children work the slide projector and read the script. They will have a good feeling of accomplishment as they create, produce, and direct their own "family show!"

6. If time permits and you have patience left, make cookies together to serve during the slide show. Good, nutritious, and made without a mixer are Oatmeal Crispies.

OATMEAL CRISPIES

1 cup melted margarine	1½ cups flour
1 cup brown sugar	1 tsp. salt
1 cup white sugar	1 tsp. soda
2 eggs, well beaten	3 cups quick-cooking oats (we
1 tsp. vanilla	have used regular oats too)

Mix together melted margarine and sugar; add eggs and vanilla; beat well. Add sifted dry ingredients. Add oatmeal (and nuts if desired). Mix well. Drop by teaspoonfuls onto greased cookie sheets and criss-cross with a fork dipped into flour. Bake at 350° for 10 minutes. Makes about 5 dozen.

(We have made this recipe for our children cutting the sugar in half and adding wheat germ for a small part of the flour—perhaps ¼ cup. They are definitely more nutritious made this way, and our children will eat them—although they like them better with all the sugar!)

When there are no slides or videos, have a Picture Show!
1. Substitute pictures for slides.
2. Arrange pictures on a table, a sheet, or in a book.
3. Write a script to go with the pictures.
4. Present a picture show complete with script, cookies, and home-made humor to family or friends.

IDEA #3—SEND A STORY TO FRIENDS

Once the Arps received a most creative gift from very special friends. It was treasured because it was a gift of themselves and their time. We thought it was such a good idea that we wanted to pass it on to you as a Children's Day activity. The only materials necessary are a tape recorder and a blank tape or blank paper.

Here is what the Arps and their three sons received.

Dear Arps,
    Open only when you are alone as a family and have at least an hour to spare!

Love,
Clark and Ann

An "old" parchment was unrolled, and it contained the following story.

A Secret Seven Story for You to Finish . . .

Once upon a time in the land of Walwyth (pronounced "wall-with") there was a very great and good king who had a lovely wife as queen and three handsome sons. The king and his wife helped many people. One time when they returned from a long trip, they brought each son a gift:

To the eldest son, they gave a tiny seahorse,

To the middle son, they gave a jeweled knife, and

To the youngest son, they gave a many-colored glass.

(The secret of these gifts was that each contained special powers because they were given in love by friends who cared!)

There was peace in the land where the young princes lived, but in the neighboring lands there was war. Sometimes bad men sneaked into Walwyth and did evil deeds. Usually these raiders were caught and punished by the king's guards, but one afternoon when the princes were out riding their ponies and practicing with their bows and arrows, something unexpected happened.

The king had sent all his soldiers away on an urgent mission, and some raiders disguised as palace guards rode right into the castle courtyard, robbed the king's treasure chest, and kidnapped the king and queen!

When the princes returned, they heard loud crying. Soon they learned what had happened and discovered that there was no one to pursue the robbers and rescue the king and queen!

The youngest son said, "*We* must go after them at once!"

The second son said, "*Yes,* but first we should quickly pack a lunch and make ready because we don't know how long it will take to rescue them!"

The oldest son, with a serious expression on his face, gave the orders for all to be made ready. He had the ponies fed and a pack horse brought to carry the tent, extra supplies, and food for the princes' dogs who always went with them.

When all was ready, the princes knelt in a circle and asked God for wisdom and protection. Then they mounted their ponies and at a full gallop rode in the direction the kidnappers had gone. Each had tucked his magic gift safely in a pocket.

The tracks of the raiders were clear, and the princes followed them steadily toward the coast of Mania. There must have been about twenty in the raiding party, and one was probably a giant! His horse's tracks were as big as a dinner plate and sunk deep into the ground because of the weight. Other tracks showed that wild dogs ran alongside the raiders' horses.

31

How were they going to rescue their parents and get the treasure back?

> We'd love to hear the end you give this adventure!

> —Clark and Ann

Along with the unfinished story, for each child there was a special gift with a clue:

> . . . to Jarrett— a tiny seahorse
> "Because of interest and need . . ."
> . . . to Joel— a jeweled knife (letter-opener)
> "Just for fun and for good . . ."
> . . . to Jonathan—a multicolored glass
> "So he'll always have a glass and sometimes a boat . . ."

The Arps had a fun family time as together they fantasized their own fairy tale. Their friends had interwoven each boy's personality into the story. Later, for a family night activity, they reread the story and continued it—via tape—for their friends, still leaving it open-ended and unfinished.

To send a story from your family, pick a family you love and want to remember.

1. Together discuss each child in the chosen family and pick out one special thing about his or her personality that you could weave into a story of your own. For example, the Arp family remembers the Dillow children this way:

> Tommy—"sports-minded and loves to eat"
> Robin—"could be called Miss Sunshine—optimistic and happy"
> Joy—"excellent gymnast and a real organizer"
> Niki—"laid back diplomat"

2. Look through your house for little things you could use as gifts and weave into the story—pencils, rocks, toy boats, planes, or cars. You can use *anything!*

3. Discuss and create a plot using your friends' personalities in the story. Get the story going and then leave it unfinished for them to continue.

4. Write the story—You could burn the edges of the paper to make it look old. Or make a tape.

5. Wrap presents and all and get it ready for mailing. Take it to the post office and send it on its way.

6. Return home for cookies and juice and lots of fun speculating on what your friends will say when they get your special package!

Indoor Fun—Planning Needed

IDEA #1—LET'S CROCHET

Crochet (or loop by hand) a chain-stitch picture to adorn kitchen wall, child's room, or to give to Grandmother for Christmas.

Materials needed:

1. Yarn—four to six colors, perhaps white, red, orange, yellow, green, or blue

2. Crochet hooks—medium size, J or H

3. Glue or glue sticks

4. Fabric for back of picture—a tightly woven material of neutral shade is best

Activity:

1. Teach the children to chain stitch.

2. Help them make chains of different colors and different lengths.

3. Decide what pictures the children want to create—a house and flowers, a sailboat, an animal, a design. Do a simple picture the first time.

4. Help children cut chains the right length for the pictures. The ends will be loose, but when they are glued down there will be no problem.

5. Glue cut chains onto fabric to create a picture or design.

Don't panic, it's *really* simple. A five-year-old can learn to chain-stitch, and once your child learns you'll probably have chains as long as jump ropes!

Chain Stitch

1. Pass hook under yarn and catch yarn with hook (see diagram 1). This is called yarn over hook.

2. Draw yarn through loop on hook (diagram 2). Do not work tightly. One chain stitch is completed.

3. Continue to yarn over and draw through a new loop (diagram 3) for the number of chain stitches required. Keep thumb and forefinger near the stitch you are working on. This keeps the chain from twisting.

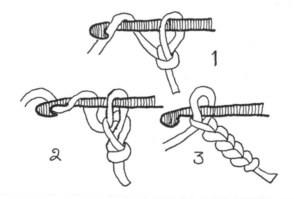

Try "yarn looping"—it's even simpler. Make a slipknot at one end of the yarn (see diagram 1).

Make a loop to the left of the slipknot. Put new loop through the original loop and pull snugly on the new loop (diagram 2).

Continue in this manner, keeping the working loop on the right large enough to put the new loop through. When the yarn is used up (or is long enough) put the end through the last loop and pull tight. This is like crocheting but without the hook!

IDEA #2—CREATIVE COOKING

Part I—*Raggedy Ann Salad Luncheon*
Morning activity: Cook Easy Peanut Butter Cookies or Sugar Cook-

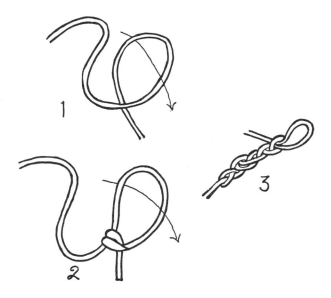

ies and make Raggedy Ann Salad. Both of these cookie recipes are simple and can be made without a mixer.

EASY PEANUT BUTTER COOKIES

1 cup peanut butter   1 egg, beaten
1 cup sugar

Mix ingredients together and drop by spoonfuls onto a cookie sheet. If you prefer, shape into balls and pat down with a fork. Bake at 375° for 10 minutes. (Believe it or not, there is no flour.)

SUGAR COOKIES

1 cup sugar   ½ tsp. cream of tartar
¾ cup salad oil   ½ tsp. soda
1 egg, beaten   ½ tsp. salt
2 cups flour   ½ tsp. to 1 tsp. vanilla

Mix sugar, oil, and egg. Sift together dry ingredients and add to sugar mixture. Add vanilla, roll in balls, and flatten a little. Put on cookie sheet and flatten with a fork, criss-crossing the fork design. Bake at 350° for 10 minutes. Sprinkle the tops with sugar.

RAGGEDY ANN SALAD

Body .... fresh or canned peach half
Arms and legs .... small celery sticks
Head .... half of hard-cooked egg
Eyes, nose, shoes, buttons ..... raisins, nuts
Mouth .... piece of a cherry or a red hot
Hair .... grated yellow cheese
Skirt .... ruffled leaf lettuce (hide tuna salad under lettuce skirt if desired)

Afternoon activity: Enjoy a wonderful lunch together. Perhaps the children will want to make place cards for the table or have candles to make it special. After lunch, take a "nature hike" around the neighborhood. (This is good for working off the calories put on by the cookies!) Give each child a bag and let him collect leaves, wildflowers, weeds, stones, mosses, and other collectable treasures. If you feel extra creative, upon returning from the neighborhood hike, provide glue and paper and let the children shape their collected "treasures" into a nature-hike collage.

Part II—*Make-Ahead Mixes*

One of the fun (and useful!) things to teach our children is how to plan ahead. On this cooking day the children will make two mixes that they will be able to use several times.

SIX-WEEK BRAN MUFFINS
(Good for breakfast, lunch, or dinner.)

3 cups All Bran cereal	2 eggs
1 cup boiling water	2½ cups flour
½ cup margarine	2½ tsp. soda
½ quart buttermilk	1 tsp. salt
¾ cup honey	

Bring water to boiling point; add shortening and All Bran. Set aside to cool or cool with buttermilk. Beat honey and eggs together and add to All Bran mixture. Mix dry ingredients and gradually add to liquid mixture. Bake in greased muffin tins at 350° for 25 minutes. May use at once or store batter in refrigerator up to six weeks. Yield: 36 muffins.

FROSTED FRUIT COCKTAIL
(Can be used as salad, dessert, or base for punch. Perfect on hot summer days. Keeps forever in freezer.)

3 medium bananas, mashed	2 lemons, juiced and strained
½ cup sugar (can be omitted)	(or ⅓ cup lemon juice)
1 can (1 cup) crushed	2 cups orange juice
pineapple in heavy syrup	2 cups ginger ale or Sprite
(use fruit and juice)	

Mix in order given. Freeze in a clean, ½-gallon milk carton or other container. Take out of freezer about ½ hour before serving. Serve in bowls when slushy. Return unused portion to freezer.

To use as punch base: Put frozen mixture in a large bowl, let thaw some, and then pour 3 to 4 bottles ginger ale over it, stirring some to break up the frozen mixture. Best punch we've ever had!

For lunch on this Children's Day you can use the bran muffins and cook Tuna Patties, a children's favorite. The Frosted Fruit Cocktail will go in the freezer to be used the next day.

TUNA PATTIES

(One of our children's favorite dishes to fix alone when Mom and Dad are out on a date.)

1 can tuna fish (7½-oz. can)   1 egg
10–12 Ritz crackers   salt and pepper

Drain tuna fish and then mix all ingredients in bowl. Form into 3 patties and fry in small amount of oil until brown on both sides. Serve with catsup!

Serve Tuna Patties hot with Bran Muffins fresh from the oven (we love them with butter and honey). Carrot sticks will make the lunch complete. Enjoy, enjoy!

If your children aren't ready for slide and art shows, sending short stories, or gourmet cooking, don't despair. The next few pages contain some ideas for creative Children's Day activities for preschool children.

PRESCHOOL CHILDREN

Outdoor Fun

Remember that tiny tots tire easily, so we need to take into consideration their endurance level (and Mom's too). Mornings are the best time for little ones, so plan activities for early in the day. Children's Day for toddlers may consist of an excursion in the morning and a nap in the afternoon (maybe for Mom too!).

IDEA #1—BACKYARD CIRCUS

This is great for a birthday party or a no-reason-at-all party.

It may require two weeks—one Children's Day to plan, make invitations, and prepare; and one Children's Day for the actual party.

PLANNING AND PREPARATION

Have on hand the following:
1. Balloons
2. Washable color markers
3. Animal cookies
4. Large boxes (from grocery store)
5. Finger paint
6. Wallpaper scraps, contact paper, etc.
7. Cake mix
8. String
9. Ice-cream cones

Make an invitation list. Then, a good rule of thumb is to have one helper (older child, teen, or other mom) for every five children. Also, keep the circus party to no more than an hour and a half—for instance, from ten to eleven-thirty.

For invitations, write on an inflated balloon and let your child decorate with color markers. Let the air out and send or deliver in the neighborhood. Be sure to tell each prospective guest to dress as a favorite performer and to bring a favorite wild, stuffed animal friend.

Sure to be a hit at any circus party are Clown Cupcakes! We suggest making the cupcakes the week before and freezing them. Then the morning of the party decorate them with your children's help—or let them decorate them with your help. Use your imagination or the following recipe.

CLOWN CUPCAKES

CAKE: Bake 1 package (18.5 oz.) any flavor layer cake in paper baking cups. Cool.

FROSTING: Prepare butter cream frosting.

⅓ cup soft butter or margarine
3 cups confectioners sugar

1½ tsp. vanilla
about 2 tsp. milk

Blend butter and sugar. Stir in vanilla and milk. Beat until smooth and/or spreading consistency.

Frost tops of half of the cupcakes. Remove paper cups from remaining cupcakes and frost sides of each. Invert on frosted cupcakes and frost "tops."

TO MAKE CLOWNS: Use pointed ice-cream cone on cupcake for hat, coconut for hair, sliced almonds or raisins for eyes, and red cinnamon candies for nose and mouth. Insert small candy wafers for ears. (Makes 15 clowns. This does *not* mean you must have 15 children!)

PAINTBRUSH COOKIES

Start with your favorite sugar cookie recipe rolled and cut but unbaked, or packaged, unbaked refrigerator cookie dough. You can also use packaged animal crackers, but the "paint" recipe is a little different.

You will also need as many cups and small paintbrushes as you have colors.

PAINT (for 4 colors)
2 egg yolks   food coloring
½ tsp. water

Blend egg yolk and water together. Divide into cups and add food coloring. Use small, clean paintbrushes to paint the unbaked cookies. Add more water if "paint" becomes too dry. Bake in a 400° oven for 6 to 8 minutes, or as directed on recipe.

NO-BAKE VERSION PAINT
(for use with animal crackers)

Make paint with evaporated milk, a little sugar, and food coloring. Allow cookies to dry before eating.

CIRCUS DAY

Decorate large cardboard boxes as cages for transporting "wild" stuffed animals. Almost anything can be used to decorate—finger paint, color markers, tempera paints, leftover pieces of wallpaper or contact paper. If you're really clever, put wheels on the boxes, or tie the boxes together with string! But either way, fun is in store for your preschoolers as they give their favorite animals a ride.

Have on hand an old white sheet and some color markers. As each child arrives, let him/her draw a favorite circus animal on the sheet. You may want to add the children's names to their art work, or have them do it if they can. Save the sheet as a reminder of the party. It also can be covered with clear plastic and used as a tablecloth.

Then have a miniature circus. Rope off circus rings in the yard with rope, string, the garden hose, or whatever you can find. Each ring can be a performance area for costumed guests. One ring could feature singers; another, acrobats or dancers; another, jugglers. A happy music cassette adds to the atmosphere. After the performance, serve clown cupcakes, cookies, and juice.

IDEA #2—A TRIP TO THE ZOO

  7:00 Mom gets up and has her Quiet Time, adding a prayer for sunshine.

  8:00 Children rise and shine. (If your children are like ours, they may already have been up and "shining" for some time!)

Eat a light breakfast. Talk about animals you will see and maybe read the story of Noah and the ark from Genesis.

9:00 Make the lunch. This is every bit as much a part of the day as is the actual visit to the zoo. We split up the preparations, including:

—making lemonade or gathering everyone's favorite flavor of juice.

—preparing the sandwiches

—washing the fruit

—loading the picnic basket

9:45 Drive or take the bus to the zoo.

10:30 Visit the animals. If you brought paper and crayons, let the children draw live portraits of their favorite animals.

12:00 Lunch and visit. Keep the conversation going with lively questions.

12:45 Finish visiting the animals.

2:00 Head back home!

3:45 Bathe, rest, clean up for supper.

6:00 This is another good night for a slow cooker dinner! Or splurge and order your favorite take-out dinner. Two of our favorites are Chinese and pizza.

Indoor Fun

IDEA #1—CREATIVE CLAY DAY

This activity is quite versatile. Older children enjoy it too, making it an excellent choice if you have children in both age groups. Children of all ages (even moms!) enjoy the sensation of working with modeling clay, and the end product is limited only by age, time, and creativity. Here are two economical recipes you can make at home.

CREATIVE CLAY

1 cup cornstarch   1¼ cups cold water
2 cups baking soda
   (1-lb. package)

Stir starch and soda together. Mix in cold water and stir over heat until mixture has consistency of mashed potatoes. Turn onto a plate and cover with a damp cloth until cool enough to handle.

Then knead. Use immediately or store in an airtight container. This dough has a smooth consistency. It is good for ornaments, modeling, or pottery. It can be rolled thin and cut with cookie cutters. Dries at room temperature in three days or you can dry it in a 200° oven.

FAVORITE PLAY DOUGH

2 cups flour	2 cups water
1 cup salt	2 Tbsp. salad oil
4 tsp. cream of tartar	food coloring

Cook over medium heat until soft, lumpy ball forms. It happens quickly! Knead for a few minutes until dough is smooth. Store in airtight container. Dough can be frozen and refrozen several times.

Why not use Christmas cookie cutters with your dough and make Christmas tree decorations for your family and for Christmas gifts?

Another suggestion is to make little figures (like Fisher Price people) for the nativity scene—they can be quite rustic. Let them dry and then paint them (use tempera paints). Pack them away safely. Then before Christmas take a walk through the woods and pick up moss, roots, acorns, sticks, stones—anything of interest. Bring them home and, on a piece of plywood, construct your own nativity scene. Our children collected extra items for their grandparents and built another one for them.

Years later it is still special to set up our little nativity people! They bring great memories of Christmases past, and also of the summer when we made them. Our little people would win no artistic award, but somehow the things our children made when they were younger are just too dear to replace!

Hints:

1. A coffee can lined with a plastic bag makes a good storage container for dough.

2. If you choose a recipe with no oil in it, it will dry hard and you can paint it with tempera.

3. If you leave the food coloring out while mixing, it can be added as you play.

4. Adding a flavor extract like lemon or vanilla will make the dough smell good.

5. Use waxed paper on the table as you play.

6. Varnish or shellac a finished project to preserve it.

IDEA #2—FINGER PAINTING

Another good indoor activity for Children's Day is finger painting. Here are three different ways to make the paint.

1. Finger Paints

   1 cup soap flakes
   ½ cup water
   dry tempera or food coloring

Whip flakes and water until thick and smooth. Stir in color, if desired. Use a blob on slick-finished paper.

2. Pudding Finger Paint (for types who get more paint in their mouths than on the paper)

On vinyl tablecloth, put dabs of pudding at each child's place and let them have a delicious time!

3. Would You Believe Shaving Cream?

Squirt a bit of aerosol shaving cream on paper. Add a few drops of tempera paint and you have instant finger paint.

MAKE CHILDREN'S DAY A TRADITION

In our homes, Children's Day was such fun that our children made it a summer tradition; they also asked that we implement the special day during school vacations. Whatever time you have—whether it's an hour, a morning, or a day or week—why not begin to plan now for that unique time with your children this summer? We guarantee it will be a positive step toward getting to know your children better!

CHAPTER 4

"Just-Me-and-Mom" Time

One mother of three spent two hours with her nine-year-old daughter playing games and then reading *Little Pilgrim's Progress* to her. As the two hours came to a close, the daughter said, "I wish I were an only child." She loved her brother and sister dearly, but she was saying, "Mommy, I like—and *need*—being alone with you, having your undivided attention all for me!"

Maybe our children do not often give us such clear hints of their need for time with us, but the need is there just the same.

One friend of ours, who became aware of this need in her teenage daughter, put it this way: "We have worked so much at family togetherness over the years—read so many books together, played so many games, and God has given us such a special family—that I was not aware of the importance of personal relationships being built in twos. I sense a limitation in my relationship with my daughter and can only pray that now this personal time can begin."

Let's look again at our first goal for this summer: to build deeper personal relationships with our children. One way of doing this is through Children's Day; fun times together provide a good climate for relationships to grow. But another consideration is time alone with each child—"Just-Me-and-Mom" time.

CROWDED LONELINESS

Pretend with us for a moment. You're at a neighborhood coffee and you see your best friend. You have something really important (at least, it's important to you) that you want to tell her. But she is always surrounded by other people, and the coffee time ends. How do you feel? Is it possible that your own children have such feelings when their need for time alone with Mom goes unmet?

Dr. Ross Campbell, in his excellent book *How to Really Love Your Child* (put this one on your "preparation for summer" reading list), defines "focused attention" this way: "Focused attention is giving a child our full, undivided attention in such a way that he feels without doubt that he is completely loved. That he is valuable enough in his own right to warrant parents' undistracted watchfulness, appreciation and uncompromising regard. In short, focused attention makes a child feel he is the most important person in the world in his parents' eyes."[1] Focused attention requires time—sometimes lots of it. It may even be that the time when a child desperately needs focused attention is when you feel least like giving it!

We would like to give you a head start this summer by helping you plan into your summer schedule opportunities for focused time together with each child. Of course, there will be times when your child needs you and it's *not* in your schedule, and it means giving up something you would rather do.

GETTING TO KNOW YOU

You can get to know people in a group situation, but only to a certain point. Trust comes from knowing someone, and knowing someone comes from time spent together. This is true in relationships with spouses, friends, and God.

Do you know your child's favorite color? Most-loved game? Favorite food? Hardest subject?

Time alone with a parent gives children the opportunity to increase their own self-awareness and to share their joys, fears, problems, successes, and frustrations in an atmosphere of total acceptance. What an aid to communication and what a good generation-gap preventer "Just-Me-and-Mom" times can be!

We tried to plan "Just-Me-and-Mom" times in each summer week. It varied from large blocks of time—like going to lunch—to smaller blocks of time perhaps closer together—like a fifteen-minute walk or two games of double solitaire. The key word is *flexibility*—adapting your schedule to your child's age and interest. An older child of eight or nine will require a longer period of time less frequently than a toddler, who might need ten minutes alone with you each day.

For some parents (the relaxed, hang-loose ones) it is simple to drop everything and play with their children; they naturally seize opportunities to spend time alone with them. For others the problem may be one of overscheduling and rigidity. We may miss special opportunities because we are already late for our appointment in the bathroom with Mr. Clean! If you are working outside the home, you may have to be even more creative—see our chapter for working parents for suggestions for finding time for "Just-Me-and-Mom" times. We must all reach our own balance, but the point is to have *some* time alone with each child regularly.

Don't limit "Just-Me-and-Mom" times just to moms—what about "Just-Me-and-Dad" times or "Just-me-and-Grandma" time. When Claudia's parents used to visit them in Vienna, Austria, she arranged a special "Just-Me-and-Grandma" and "Just-Me-and-Granddad" time for each of the boys. This allowed Claudia's parents to spend special time with each boy and really helped promote bonding between grandparent and grandchild.

Now to the practical—*how* to find the time. Here are some things that worked for us.

1. When a younger child is napping, take time with the older.

2. When a brother or sister is at a friend's house, seize the opportunity to spend time with one of the other children.

3. When an older child is at a summer activity, entertain the younger one at home.

4. Hire a baby-sitter for one, two, or more children, and go someplace with one child.

5. Pick a day of the week for each child, and let him/her know that on that day he/she will have a special time with you. Ask other children to cooperate and play nicely in their rooms when it is someone else's turn. (Good luck—it will work some of the time, but don't count on 100 percent!)

6. When one child has a doctor's appointment, use the time before or after to go out for a special treat.

7. Trade off children with friends.

8. One mother whose children were past the nap stage instigated a "creative-art time" (also known as personal development time). Each child was provided with art and/or craft materials and was expected to spend a certain amount of time (like an hour) alone doing a creative activity. Our friend used this time as a regroup-and-refresh time for herself. But she could also use this time every now and then to do something special with one child.

9. Another friend discovered that she had difficulty finding time to read to her third child. So she wrote in her *Priority Planner*[2] on Monday, Wednesday, and Friday at one o'clock to read to her daughter for fifteen minutes. Simply by planning it into her schedule she was able to do it.

10. With older children time alone with Mom is sometimes crowded out by Little League, pals, and other activities. The key here is to plan and persevere!

COUPONS FOR CLIPPING

One idea we used for planning those extra special "Just-Me-and-Mom" times was to make a coupon book. For several years the Arps and Dillows shared Thanksgiving dinner. To make our time special and to show our families how much we appreciated them, one year we made "I'm thankful for you" coupon books and used them for place cards for our children and husbands. Included were coupons for making Christmas cookies alone with Mom, a trip with Mom to a Christmas market, and going out for a hot chocolate date. They were such a big success that we discovered we had started a tradition, as our children asked the next Thanksgiving, "Do we get another coupon book this year?"

Because coupons helped us in creating "Just-Me-and-Mom" times, we adapted them for summertime use. The number of coupons you decide to give for the summer will vary according to your own situation. If you have six or more children, then one coupon apiece would be

above the call of duty! But if you have only one child, you may want to do one a week. If you work outside the home, it may be a challenge to find this special time; perhaps one evening each week or an afternoon on the weekend would be best. Remember to plan realistically—but do *plan*.

1. *How to Make*

When we first made these coupons it took only one hour to make four coupon books—including shopping time.

Materials needed:

Index cards

Cute stickers

Hole puncher

Yarn

Colored markers

Instructions:

Punch two holes in cards.

Decorate cards with stickers.

Write out coupons for each child, using one card for one coupon.

Tie each child's coupons together with yarn.

2. *How to Use*

Give to child at the beginning of summer. Together with your child, schedule times into the summer for each coupon. Or if you prefer, include the "date for cashing coupon" on each one.

One creative mom made recyclable coupons. She covered each with clear plastic and after each coupon was cashed, she recorded the event

on the back of the card with a permanent ink pen. Each summer when she brought out the coupons, memories of past summers were enjoyed.

We would like to share with you some summer "coupon" ideas we tried for "Just-Me-and-Mom" time.

Cooking with Mom

All of our children—boys and girls alike—really enjoyed cooking alone with us. That way one child got to crack *all* the eggs, sift *all* the flour, and decorate *all* the cookies. And best of all—there was no fighting with siblings! One friend of ours thought she was really extra creative in coming up with the idea of dividing the cookie dough in half, giving both small children a portion of dough and a cookie sheet. Thinking she had avoided all problems, she was flabbergasted upon returning to the kitchen from answering the phone to find the children waging war and throwing dough at one another!

This is not to say that cooking with more than one child has to be traumatic, but cooking alone with Mom *is* a different and safer experience.

Here are some recipes we used successfully for coupon cooking.

WACKY CAKE
(extra simple)

Preheat oven to 350°.

Into ungreased 12-x-12 pan mix the following, sifted together:

1½ cups flour	1 tsp. soda
1 cup sugar	½ tsp. salt
3 Tbsp. cocoa	

Make 3 holes in these dry ingredients. Into one put 6 tablespoons vegetable oil. Into one put 1 teaspoon vanilla. Into one put 1 tablespoon vinegar.

Then pour 1 cup cold water over all and stir with a fork until smooth. Bake at 350° for about 30 minutes.

FROSTING FOR WACKY CAKE

2 cups powdered sugar	1 tsp. vanilla
2 Tbsp. cocoa	3 Tbsp. cold liquid coffee
½ cup melted margarine	

Mix all ingredients together, leaving the coffee until last, and pour on *hot* cake.

TREASURED BALLS
(simple but fattening)

1 cup margarine
6 Tbsp. brown sugar
1 Tbsp. vanilla

1 cup semi-sweet chocolate pieces
2 cups less 4 Tbsp. sifted flour

Soften margarine. Add brown sugar and vanilla. Cream. Add semi-sweet chocolate pieces. Add flour; blend and shape into 1-inch balls. Bake on ungreased cookie sheet. Bake 15–20 minutes at 350°. Cool and roll in confectioners' sugar.

MOLASSES COOKIES
(an easy roll-out cookie for advanced beginners)

1 cup margarine
1 cup sugar
1 cup molasses

2 tsp. soda
4 Tbsp. milk
4½ cups flour

Melt margarine and mix with sugar and molasses. Sift dry ingredients and add alternately with milk to molasses mixture. Chill and then have fun rolling out! Bake at 350° on greased sheet until done (about 8–10 minutes).

You and one child can create a lunch for family members who are home. The lunch does not have to be fancy. It can be the old standbys—peanut butter and jelly, tuna, grilled cheese, or egg salad sandwiches. The point is to do it together and to spend the time alone. Allow extra time to share and talk and to have your child help.

If you want to add a gourmet look to your luncheon or are just in the mood, try Bologna and Cheese Animal Sandwiches. They are perfect for an indoor lunch or a picnic in the backyard. To make them, cut out bologna, cheese, and bread with animal cookie cutters, and stack. Serve with carrot sticks, chips, and milk (served with straws, of course!).

A Date for Two

When was the last time you and *one child* planned to go out on a "date"? (Stopping by a fast-food place with your children plus a friend and her children does not count!) We're talking about you and one child going someplace *alone* together. A date usually involves an extended time commitment, so perhaps you would do this only once a summer with each child. More often would be super, but we suggest a coupon so you'll do it at least once.

Where can you go on a date? Of course, it depends on where you live, but here are some things you might be able to do with your children for "Just-Me-and-Mom" times.

1. Take public transportation (great fun in itself!) to the city.

2. Walk to a special ice-cream shop and eat a big cone (child gets a big cone, mother a small one). Then walk home. Walking is a lost art, but can be lots of fun. Try parking the car several blocks away and walking to the restaurant or ice-cream shop.

3. Ride bikes to a pretty place; stop for a "brought-along" snack; talk; share the lovely view; then ride home.

4. Go to wherever your child chooses for lunch. For small children fast foods are usually the first choice. It gets scary when they're older and begin to choose more expensive places!

5. Shop together for a special gift or a birthday card, and include time for a treat and a short talk.

Reading for Enjoyment

This coupon could provide many special "Just-Me-and-Mom" times as you and your child travel through the summer with the little Pilgrim in the book *Little Pilgrim's Progress*. Not only will both of you enjoy the book, but it will open the door to many wonderful discussions.

We have found some excellent "read-out-loud" books.

Preschoolers

1. Arch Books—Short books in poem form that teach biblical truths (Concordia)
2. *Winnie the Pooh—The House at Pooh Corner* by A. A. Milne (Dutton)
3. *Make Way for Ducklings* by Robert McClosky (Viking)
4. *Curious George* by Margaret and H. A. Rays (Houghton-Mifflin)
5. *Little Visits with God* by Jahsmann and Simon (Concordia)

A preschooler needs to have a book finished in one session, so perhaps you might pick six or eight books to read aloud this summer. Little tots love lots of pictures! You might make a special reading coupon and include a visit to the library so that the child can help select the books.

School-Age Children

1. *Little Pilgrim's Progress* by Helen L. Taylor (Moody)
2. *Little House on the Prairie* series by Laura Ingalls Wilder (Harper)

3. *Chronicles of Narnia* series by C. S. Lewis (Macmillan)

4. *Treasures of the Snow* and *Lost on the Trail* by Patricia St. John (Moody)

5. *The Boxcar Children* series by Gertrude Chandler Warner (Albert Whitman & Co)

6. *Mrs. Piggle-Wiggle* series by Betty MacDonald (Lippincott)

Shopping with Mom

What better way to end the summer and begin the school year than by shopping alone for school supplies, new clothes, or whatever is needed! We used this day to shop, have lunch, and talk about the school year ahead.

Remember, you don't need a coupon to have a "Just-Me-and-Mom" time. The coupon idea is to *insure* that you have several special times together this summer. But watch for those moments when you can snatch ten or fifteen minutes with a child to read a book, take a walk around the block, play a game like Old Maid, Go Fish, Crazy Eights, Sorry, or Mastermind, ride bikes together, or have juice and cookies together alone in the kitchen. Try it and before long your children will be asking you, "Can we have a 'Just-Me-and-Mom' time?"

Remember, building relationships continues throughout the year. At the end of the summer talk about your favorite coupon time and plan a special date for fall, winter, and spring.

CHILDREN WON'T WAIT

It's the special times together with our children—both the impromptu and the planned—that build your relationship for the future. The day-in, day-out times are vital. Helen Young, a mother of four grown children, writes clearly of the importance of each day in a child's life in this poem.

Children Won't Wait

There is a time to show my child . . .
God in earth and sky and flower, to teach them to wonder and
    reverence.
There is a time to leave the dishes, to swing him in the park,
To run a race, to draw a picture, to catch a butterfly, to give him
    happy comradeship.
There is a time to point the way, to teach his infant lips to pray.
To teach his heart to love God's Word, to love God's day . . . for
    children don't wait.

There is a time to share with him my best in attitudes—a love of life,
    a love of God, a love of family.
There is a time to answer his questions, all his questions, because
    there may come a time when he will not want my answers.

There is a time to watch him bravely go to school, to miss him
underfoot,
There is a time to teach him independence, responsibility,
self-reliance,
To be firm but friendly, to discipline with love.
For soon, so soon, there will be a time to let him go, the apron
strings untied . . . for children won't wait.

There is a time to treasure every fleeting moment of his
childhood—the precious years to inspire and train.
A time to understand that an hour of concern today may save years of
heartache tomorrow.
The house will wait, the dishes will wait, the new room will wait . . .
but children don't wait.[3]

CHAPTER 5

Communication
Is Contagious

The Arps' out-of-town company quota had been heavy and Claudia was exhausted. But she was happy to be back to just the family again and couldn't wait to get reorganized. There was so much to do to get the house back in order!

Her plan of attack was to begin in the largest disaster zone—Jonathan's room. Once there, she saw her best winter leather gloves—or rather, one glove—on Jonathan's floor. How did her best glove end up on his floor? Certainly he had been into things that were off limits—imagine pulling out gloves in the summertime!

Without seeking any more evidence, Claudia called Jonathan in for sentencing. "Jonathan, what is my best glove doing on *your* floor—and where is the other one?"

Her anger was vented, and the case was closed! That is, it was until she saw the look on Jonathan's face. What if he wasn't guilty despite the circumstantial evidence, Claudia wondered. Slowly it dawned on her that the crime could have been committed by any one of the many children who had passed through their home recently. But she had convicted and sentenced Jonathan without any room for defense.

Now to the Dillow household. It was the last week of school, and backpacks filled with books, supplies, lunches, jump ropes, and glasses were finally assembled and loaded on the backs of the children. Kisses, reminders, and good-bye waves sent them traipsing to the bus stop. Fifteen minutes later Joy burst through the front door, shouting, "Mommy, I forgot to feed Tinkerbell!" (her pet hamster).

Responding with irritation and frustration, Linda snapped, "Joy, you'll miss your bus and be late for school. Tinkerbell will easily survive six hours without food!" Joy was in tears, and Mom was angry that she'd gotten angry.

MOUTH MUZZLE NEEDED!

Have you ever wanted to bite off your tongue, zip your mouth, or retract your words? Why is it so hard to speak kindly to those we love the most? We don't plan to be offensive, irritating, and unloving. Many times we just don't think about how we're coming across.

We read about one young mother with nine children, all under age ten (made us want to take a nap!). The children were all bickering and the mother said, "Children, children, don't you know that the Bible says to be kind to one another?" Looking around the room, the eldest child said, "But, Mommy, only the family is here!"

Somehow it's easier to speak kindly to those we hardly know or only see socially—like the Tupperware lady, the hair stylist, or the checker at the grocery store. We've listened to ourselves and sadly admitted that we said things to our children we'd never say to a friend. Like—"Your room is like a pig pen! What a mess!" (Imagine saying that to a friend whose home was not as tidy as it could be!) Or, "You're not going out looking like that, are you?" Or, "Close the door! We don't live in a barn!"

We know that the singsong chant from childhood—"Sticks and stones may break my bones, but words will never hurt me"—is untrue. Words can and do hurt! We know this, and yet we still say hurtful words to our children. We hate to admit it, but even now with all of our children grown, we still from time to time say inappropriate things.

The words we say are important, but equally important is *when* we say them. Your child has just cut his foot. He is in tears, jumping up and down on the uninjured foot. Be assured: this is not the ideal time to discuss with him his failure to practice the piano!

What we say is important, and *when* we say it is important. There is one more important and often overlooked factor: *how* we say it! Would you believe that a communication study revealed that the words we speak account for only 7 percent of the total message? Fifty-five percent of the message is our nonverbal communication (the stares, glares, and pulling of hairs!). The tone of voice is 38 percent of the message (that includes the sighs, shrieks, and nags). We may even be saying the right words, but the shrug, glare, or nagging bossiness of voice may be giving a totally different message![1]

One of our goals is to build better communication with our children, but what child wants to open up to a mom who talks about practicing the piano when he's in mortal pain, convicts him without a trial over one glove, or makes negative comments and listens with closed ears?

It is easy for negative communication to become a habit; before we know what's happened, we're in a negative thinking pattern—and holding! To help eliminate wrong thinking patterns and move the communication gears forward, schedule into your summer weeks some of the communication activities included here. They will be an encouragement to you in learning to listen, in identifying problem areas in your child's life, and in attacking the problem and not the person. Your child, too, will be encouraged to express feelings and progress toward a good communication code.

ARE YOU LISTENING?

How often do we parents interrupt our children when they are telling us something to impart "important" information like, "You really need a haircut," "Stand up straight," or "Don't chew your gum like that"? Often we rob ourselves of in-depth, meaningful conversations by bringing up trivial things at a time when our children are really opening their hearts to us.

We were surprised to read in Norman Wright's book, *Communication: Key to Your Marriage* that it is estimated that most people hear only 20 percent of what is said to them. The book gave these suggestions for listening.

1. One cannot listen intently unless one's mouth is shut.

2. Listening effectively means that when someone is talking, you are not thinking about what you are going to say when the other person stops.

3. Listening is more than politely waiting for your turn to speak.[2]

In our efforts to become better listeners we have tried several things we think you'll be interested in.

First, we asked our children questions designed to give us more insight into them as people and concentrated on really listening to their responses. Some of the open-ended statements we used were:

1. If I had three wishes, I'd wish for . . .
2. My favorite food is . . .
3. My favorite color is _____, because . . .
4. My pet peeve is . . .

5. My favorite book is . . .
6. The thing I like most about my family is . . .
7. When I grow up, I'd like to be . . .
8. My best friend is . . .
9. Sometimes I feel . . .
10. If I were a parent, I would . . .
11. I worry about . . .
12. What I like best about myself is . . .

Maybe you'll want to plan a special "Just-Me-and-Mom" time this summer to use these (or your own) open-ended questions to get to know your children better and to concentrate on really listening to them. This could also be adapted to a Children's Day activity, teaching your children to take turns, to communicate, and to listen.

ARE YOU A JUGGLER?

There will be planned "Just-Me-and-Mom" times for talking and listening, but be on the alert for other important listening times. Suppose one child comes into the kitchen. Rather than trying to carry on a conversation while doing a juggling act, take a break, sit down, and focus all your attention on that one child. It is sad to say that most mothers only look at their children eyeball to eyeball when they are correcting them or telling them something they really want them to hear. How long does it take to stop and listen and give focused attention—ten or fifteen minutes, or less. And after the child has recovered from the shock of having your undivided attention, he/she will really enjoy it!

With older children it's harder to listen because they're in and out or on the phone—in constant motion. So persevere and plan times for listening. Expand the idea of the open-ended questions, adapting them for older children or teenagers. For example, ask a question and then let your child ask you one. Start with nonthreatening subjects and move on to deeper things.

1. My goal in life is . . .
2. I like being (or look forward to being) a teenager because . . .
3. I know God is real because . . .
4. The person I respect most is . . .
5. The reason I respect this person most is . . .
6. A good teacher should . . .

7. The thing I like best about myself is . . .
8. The thing I would most like to change about myself is . . .
9. Being a Christian means . . .
10. When I am a parent, I will . . .

You'll be amazed at the penetrating questions *you* may have to answer, but it is really worth it.

ON THEIR BACKS OR ON THEIR TEAM?

We once heard someone say that the way to be a successful mother is to be able to get behind the child's eyeballs and to identify with him/her. In *Between Parent and Child,* Dr. Haim Ginott tells the story of a boy named Eric and his mother, who was trying to do this very thing.

Eric, age nine, came home full of anger. His class was scheduled to go for a picnic, but it was raining. Mother decided to use a new approach. She refrained from clichés that in the past had only made things worse, like "There is no use crying over rained-out picnics." "There will be other days for fun." "I didn't make it rain, you know, so why are you angry at me?"

To herself she said, "My son has strong feelings about missing the picnic. He is disappointed. He is sharing his emotions. I can best help him by showing understanding and respect for his feelings." To Eric she said:

MOTHER: You seem very disappointed.
ERIC: Yes.
MOTHER: You wanted very much to go to this picnic.
ERIC: I sure did!
MOTHER: You had everything ready and then the rain came.
ERIC: Yes, that's exactly right.

There was a moment of silence and then Eric said, "Oh, well, there will be other days."[3]

We're sure Eric felt his mother was really on his team that day. Do our children feel we are "on their teams" instead of "on their backs"?

Like Eric's mother, we need to be sensitive to our children's feelings and identify with them. With some children, this is easier said than done. If you have the a "Timmy the Turtle," encourage him to come out of his shell by trying some of the following suggestions.

Puppets

Puppets are perfect for younger children who—because of embarrassment, shyness, stubbornness, or whatever reason—will not open up. It is easier for them to express themselves through a puppet than to tell you things face to face. The talkative child also will enjoy making a personal puppet friend and talking to you via the puppet.

Of course, you can buy a puppet at any toy store, but why not have a "Communication Children's Day" and make your own. Then talk through the questions on pages 60–61 together via puppets. These puppets are easy to make and require very few materials. Give it a try!

FINGER PUPPETS

Materials needed:

1. Old gloves—rubber or fabric (or sacrifice a new rubber glove for the cause of communication)

2. Felt-tip pen

Instructions:

Cut one finger off old glove. Decorate with felt-tip pen. Place over finger and wiggle.

SOCK PUPPETS

Materials needed:

1. Old socks (if your washing machine "eats" socks like ours does, you should have several "solo" socks)

2. Fabric and yarn scraps

3. Buttons and other trims

4. Glue or glue stick

5. Felt-tip pens

6. Scissors

7. Needle and thread

63

Instructions:

Put sock over hand. Glue or sew button eyes where your fist fits into sock. Add a felt tongue or ears or a hat, or draw the face with felt pens. If you want, you can create a whole "family" of puppets.

BOX PUPPETS

Materials needed:

1. Small individual cereal boxes (the kind that are supposed to keep kids from fighting over the cereal)
2. Paper and yarn scraps
3. Crayons or felt-tip pens
4. Scissors
5. Glue or glue stick
6. Knife

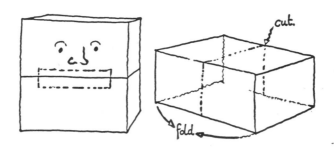

Instructions:

Do not open cereal box by tearing off end. An adult opens by cutting with a sharp knife across the center and down both sides. Fold on remaining fourth side. (See sketch.) Decorate with scraps and crayons. Insert hand and move fingers to make puppet talk.

SACK PUPPETS

Materials needed:
1. Lunch-size paper bag
2. Scraps of fabric, paper, yarn, felt
3. Glue
4. Scissors
5. Crayons, felt-tip pens, or paints

Instructions:

Glue or draw face on bottom of bag. The fold in the bag is used for the mouth opening. Add yarn for hair and whiskers. You may want to add a paper hat or ears. Let your child create!

"JUST-ME-AND-MOM" PUPPET TIME

One summer when the older Arp boys were at Boy Scouts, Claudia and Jonathan had a special time together with "Hans" the puppet. Jonathan shared all about his day and talked to his mother through Hans. In this way Claudia learned much about her son and his deep feelings.

Why not plan a "Just-Me-and-Mom" Puppet Time with your child? It can be a time to share experiences through puppets, make up a play about people you know, answer questions (like the ones on pages 60–61), or just talk about what happened that day. Most younger children enjoy this new way of talking with Mom.

"I AM ME"

An excellent way to help children express their feelings is the children's activity book *My Book about Me* by Dr. Seuss and Roy McKie (Random House).

THE UNGAME

"What kind of animal would you like to be?" "Describe a happy home." "What would you like to invent to make life better?" These are some of the questions asked in a fun game that has helped us to really get to know our older children better. It's called the Ungame, and it can be played as a family or alone with one child. This is an excellent idea for a rainy Children's Day, or it can be a special "Just-Me-and-Mom" time. There are special cards that can be bought separately for parents and teenagers, spiritual questions, and also marriage enrichment cards (for after the kids are in bed). The game can be bought at many Christian book stores.

ATTACK THE PROBLEM, NOT THE PERSON

It's easy to talk around issues and verbally attack those around us—those we love the most. To help at our homes for a period of time we chose a communication "tip of the week" and then tried to apply it. It helped us break down some negative patterns. Here are three examples.

WEEK ONE—*No "you" statements*.

Often, sentences that begin with "you" attack the other person; "I" statements are much safer. They tell your feelings without leveling charges against another person. "*You* never take the trash out!" "*You* are irresponsible!" "*You* are so messy!"

The first week we tried this communication rule there were a lot of uncompleted sentences, but there were two happier households. We found ourselves beginning to say, "I would appreciate it if you would take out the trash."

WEEK TWO—*Express your feelings and really listen to the other person.*

You know how it is when you want to discuss a difficult issue and you just don't know how to begin? We can get into an argument before we ever get to the issue! This rule has really helped us in getting the issue out in the open and attacking *it* instead of each other. We begin by stating how we feel. For instance, "I am frustrated . . . disappointed . . . anxious." This helps us state our feelings and our position without attacking.

Claudia remembers trying this communication rule with one of her budding teenagers.

"Many times our twelve-year-old answered me with a note of sarcasm—you know, just on the borderline and irritating. Sometimes I'd grin and bear it, and other times I'd explode, 'Don't be sarcastic with me!'

"Well, one day he did it again, so I said with a calm and sane voice, 'Let me tell you how I feel. I feel angry and frustrated when you respond in this way to me.'

"With a look of shock on his face, he said, 'Gee, Mom, I'm sorry. I didn't mean to be ugly.'

"What a difference—no confrontation and good communication was restored. Later I had to correct him again about something else that required real firmness. In an attempt to identify with him after I had corrected him, I said, 'Hey, I'm still on your team.'

"He replied, 'Yes, Mom, but you just benched me!'

"I responded, 'Happens to the best of players!'" Confrontation completed, but communication still open!

WEEK THREE—*Say positive things!*

Every day each family member tries to say at least one nice thing to each of the other members of the family.

YOUR COMMUNICATION CODE

Why not take a Family Night or Children's Day to work out your own family communication guidelines and start having a communication "rule of the week" at your house this summer? Remember, good communication helps us attack the problem instead of the person.

One family decided on ten communication rules to use for ten weeks during the summer. They wrote the rules on slips of paper and put them in a jar. On a designated day each week, they drew out that week's rule. It was a fun family venture, and communication was improved.

We challenge you to improve communication with your children this summer. Use puppets, questions, games, or whatever fits the needs and age level of your children. You may just find that by summer's end good communication is contagious at your house!

CHAPTER 6

Summer Strategies
for Self-Esteem

Several young people were asked to write ten conclusions for the sentence beginning, "I am . . ." One wrote, "I am ugly. I am not very smart. I am sad." Another wrote, "I am a child of God. I am happy. I am a good painter." What would your children's responses be?

One of our children came home one day and told about a new friend in her class. Most of the children didn't want to be her friend because she looked different—she was a head taller than the others in the class. A friend laughingly told us about her thirty-year-old husband who only wears long-sleeved shirts (even in summer) because as a high school student he was teased about his skinny arms. Another friend remembers being called "stupid" by her aunt. It's amazing how we remember seemingly insignificant statements made years ago.

BEAUTY AND BRAINS

One of our favorite books, James Dobson's *Hide or Seek,* contends that the two most admired qualities in our society are beauty and brains. (Perhaps for boys, brawn could be added.) The child who is naturally attractive and has above-average intelligence often has smooth sailing through life. He or she has built-in advantages over the tall ten-year-old girl, the skinny-armed boy, and the child who is a slow learner.

The whole thing is grossly unfair! Why should our appearance and brain power or achievement orientation have so much to do with how we see ourselves and how others see us? We try to teach our children that it's the "inner qualities" that count, yet "beauty and brains" is the mes-

69

sage they hear from all sides. They need to hear a different message from us!

The first thing our children need to hear from us is how God sees them. Psalm 139:13–16 is an excellent passage to share with children of all ages.

> You made all the delicate, inner parts of my body, and knit them together in my mother's womb. Thank you for making me so wonderfully complex! It is amazing to think about. Your workmanship is marvelous—and how well I know it. You were there while I was being formed in utter seclusion! You saw me before I was born and scheduled each day of my life before I began to breathe. Every day was recorded in your Book! (TLB)

Be sure to emphasize the words *wonderfully complex, marvelous,* and *amazing.* We parents are God's tools to help our children see and accept God's viewpoint of their appearance, abilities, intelligence—of their total being. God says the issue is not how many talents or how much intelligence we have, but faithfulness with the abilities and intelligence He has given us (1 Cor. 4:1–2).

A sizable proportion of a child's self-concept emerges from the way he thinks his parents "see" him. When a child is convinced he is greatly loved and respected by his parents, he is inclined to accept his own worth as a person.

Understanding the problem is important; realizing that each child needs our love and admiration is important; but what can we as mothers *do* this summer to help our children see their uniqueness and accept themselves?

Have an "Inner Beauty" Discussion Time

Why not plan a Children's Day or a family night to set personal goals for inner beauty?[1]

The key verse is 1 Samuel 16:7 (TLB): "But the Lord said to Samuel, 'Don't judge by a man's face or height . . . I don't make decisions the way you do! Men judge by outward appearance, but I look at a man's thoughts and intentions.' "

1. INNER BEAUTY/OUTER BEAUTY

Begin the time together by talking about two kinds of beauty. Identify what makes a person outwardly attractive (good looks, nice clothes, strong body, good figure, etc.). Then help family members define characteristics of inner beauty (love for others, kindness, patience, willingness to help others, etc.).

Compare God's statement in 1 Samuel 16:7 with 1 Peter 3:3–4. What do these two Bible passages say about God's view of inner and outer beauty?

2. BEAUTIFUL PEOPLE WE KNOW

Have family members identify people who have true inner beauty. Decide why family members feel these people have this special beauty.

Also name two or three people who are attractive from an outer beauty standpoint. Do inner and outer beauty sometimes go together? Why or why not? Can a person be unattractive outwardly but still have real inner beauty? Why?

3. ENJOY A FAMILY SNACK

As you eat, talk about which is best for a person to focus on every day—inner or outer beauty? Why? What would the world be like if everyone focused on outer beauty? Would the world be better or worse if everyone concentrated on inner beauty? Why?

4. PERSONAL BEAUTY PLAN

Give each person a sheet of paper. Allow time for everyone to write out *one* way he or she wants to try to be more beautiful in outward appearance. Then each person should plan for at least *two* ways to work on improving inner beauty. Decide together if you want to share your goals or keep them secret as each person's private plan.

HAVE A POSITIVE PICTURE

"Finally, brethren, whatever is true, . . . honorable, . . . pure, . . . lovely, . . . if there is any excellence and if anything worthy of praise, let your mind dwell on these things. . . . and the God of peace shall be with you" (Phil. 4:8–9). We are instructed to think about positive things. A person is a by-product of what he/she thinks about; if our children hear positive things about themselves, they will begin to think positively about themselves. The positive needs to be in their minds and in their hearts. A good place to begin is to encourage and help your children to memorize Scripture portions about how God views them (1 Sam. 16:7, 1 Pet. 3:3–4 and portions of Psalm 139 would be excellent to use).

For younger children, plan a special time to listen to Sandi Patti. *Psalty Agapeland; Sandi Patti's Friendship Company;* or *Patch the Pirate* are good tapes to use. Listen, learn the words, and sing them together. If a stereo is not readily available, learn the songs as poems. The messages of the Bill Gaither Trio's "You're Something Special" and "I Am a Promise" are fantastic and have had a tremendous impact on our children.

You're Something Special

When Jesus sent you to us
We loved you from the start
You were just a bit of sunshine
From heaven to our hearts
Not just another baby
'Cause since the world began
There's been something very special
For you in His plan
That's why He made you special
You're the only one of your kind
God gave you a body
And a bright healthy mind
He had a special purpose
That He wanted you to find
So He made you something special
You're the only one of your kind.*

I Am a Promise

I am a promise
I am a possibility—
I am a promise with a capital "P"
I can be anything God wants me to be.

You are a promise!
You are a possibility!
You are a promise with a capital "P!"
You are a great big bundle of potentiality!
And if you'll listen, you'll hear God's voice;

---

*"You're Something Special." Words by William J. and Gloria Gaither. © Copyright 1975 by William J. Gaither. All rights reserved. Used by permission. Available on Word records.

And if you're trying, He'll help you make the right choice
You're a promise to be anything He wants you to be!

You know something?
It doesn't matter what your name is,
Where you live, who your daddy is,
Or how big you are, or what you look like.
Hey, what do you look like?
Short? Tall? Are you fat, skinny,
Got holes in your tennis shoes and freckles on your nose?
It doesn't matter one bit!
You can be exactly what God wants you to be;
And He has something very special in mind for you.
It might be climbing mountains or sailing the sea,
Helping sick people get well
Or singing a song
Whatever it is you can do it!

You can go anywhere that He wants you to go,
You can be anything that He wants you to be—
You can climb the high mountain,
You can cross the wide sea,
You're a great big promise you see!

I am a promise!
I am a possibility!
I am a promise with a capital "P"
I am a great big bundle of potentiality!
And I am learning to hear God's voice and I am tryin'
To make the right choices;
I'm a promise to be anything God wants me to be!

So keep on list'ning, you'll hear God's voice,
And keep on tryin', He'll help you make the right choices—
You're a promise to be anything He wants you to be!
I'm a promise to be anything God wants me to be!
You're a promise to be anything, anything He wants you to be!*

VERBALIZE APPRECIATION

With Notes

A favorite note at our home was "Have a Happy Day! I'm so glad
Jesus gave you to me. You're so very special to God and to me. I love

---

*"I Am a Promise." Words by William J. and Gloria Gaither. © Copyright 1974 by
William J. Gaither. All rights reserved. Used by permission. Available on Word
records.

you. Mommy." Summertime is a perfect time to express love through notes dropped in a picnic lunch, hidden under a pillow, or tucked in a bathing cap. We don't write notes to get notes, but it can happen. After years of writing notes Linda received one from her eleven-year-old daughter. "Dear Mommy, I'm so glad that Jesus gave you to me for my mommy. You are so special to me. I love you. Joy."

With a Gift for No Reason

A gift could be some cute stickers, a bucket and shovel, a soccer ball, sunglasses, sugarless gum, or anything (anything cheap, that is!). The gift itself is not important; it's the message of saying, "I love you just because you're you." You could even get "artsy" and write a poem, like the one a child found attached to new colored markers.

> Because you're special and neat
> I bought for you a little treat!
> May you have fun as you draw today
> And your talent and creativity display!

The poem may not win any literary awards, but the child will feel delight in the fact that he or she is special enough to merit not only new markers but a poem too!

If poetic ability is not your strong suit, just write a note expressing your love. We used to keep several three-by-five cards handy in our kitchen cupboards, along with cute stickers. A "card" is quickly made with one of these three by five cards, a sticker, and a felt pen. It is much cheaper than buying a commercial card. Again, it is not the gift or the poem or a lovely card that is important; it's that you took the time to buy or make a small gift and express your love for your child.

Be a Secret Pal

Roses are nice
Violets aren't mean
I am so lucky cause
I'm on you're team.

—from your
secret pal

74

To emphasize how special each family member was, one summer we drew names for a "secret pal." The idea was to do something often for the secret pal (in secret). Evidences of "secret pals" were found in the above poem pinned to the refrigerator (complete with "lovely" picture!), Dad's pajamas and slippers by the bed and the sheet turned back for him, and Mom's dresser neatly cleaned. Secret pals remained secret for one week and then everyone guessed who his or her pal was.

Have a Special Person Party

How better to help one child feel special or important than by letting him/her feel like "queen or king for a day"!

One family chose to have a party in honor of their oldest son when he began his first summer job picking strawberries. Hot, bone weary, and aching from head to toe, he stumbled into the house one evening to discover posters, presents, and poems—all with his name on them. It was a party to express his family's love and to show him that they were on his team.

The walls were decorated with posters that said, "My brother is great! He wins the Strawberry Picker Award!" "We love Sam." Silly gifts had been wrapped and were stacked at his place at the table. With each gift was a poem or note to express appreciation. The meal was his favorite, the dessert extra special.

After dinner each family member gave Sam a coupon saying what they would do for him the following week: "I will empty the trash for you." "I will make your bed for one week." After dinner a slide show was given in his honor, showing pictures of his life from the first year to the present. He was the "star" for one night.

Think for a moment how you would feel if your family spent the time to plan a Special Person Party in your honor. That is exactly how each of your children or your husband would feel.

Here are some ideas for Special Person Parties.

a. Use a Children's Day this summer to plan a Special Person Party for another family member, special friend, or elderly neighbor. The day can be spent together cooking the food, making "We love you" posters, drawing pictures, wrapping silly gifts, preparing a slide show and letting the children write a script, practicing a song to sing, thinking of special things to do the following week as coupon gifts. Let your imagination run wild, or better yet, ask your children (their imagination is *already* wild) what they would like to do for the special person.

b. Use a Children's Day or "Just-Me-and-Mom" time to plan a Special Person Party for one child. The perfect time to plan this is when one child is visiting relatives or friends or is away at camp and the other children are home with you. What fun it is to plan a special surprise party for the brother or sister who is gone!

c. Choose times when Special Person Parties are in order even though it is very inconvenient for you.

> . . . when Dad worked hard on a project at work for months, and he just called to say it has all fallen through.
>
> . . . when the neighborhood kids laughed at your child because of his/her new braces and he/she says he/she's not smiling for two years.
>
> . . . when your child studied hard for his/her exam but studied the wrong things.
>
> . . . when a super summer week has been planned and your child gets the chicken pox.
>
> . . . when Mom "gracefully" trips over the sidewalk curb and breaks her ankle. *She* needs a party! (Give the book to spouse and children and mildly suggest, "It's *my* turn!")

Note: If you feel overwhelmed by "a slide show—so much work!" then don't have a slide show! We may sound redundant, but it's not how fancy, how much, or how expensive, but the fact that you cared enough to take the time to say, "I love you."

Other Ideas

For other fun and simple-to-do ideas, see Dave and Claudia Arp's book, *60 One-Minute Memory Builders*—Part One "You Are Special." If you are a single and/or working parent, these minute "ideas" will help you find the time to let your child know he/she is special.

READ SPECIAL BOOKS ABOUT SELF-IMAGE

There are many books available on the subject of self-image that can help us help our children.

Hide or Seek by Dr. James Dobson (Revell) is one we cannot recommend highly enough! Put it at the top of your list of books to read. The book explicitly explains the problem of self-image and gives great encouragement to parents. *Your Child's Self-Esteem* by Dorothy Corkille Briggs (Dolphin) is another good book for parents. Others include: *The Blessing* by Gary Smalley and John Trent (Thomas Nelson); *How to Really Love Your Child* by Dr. Ross Campbell (Victor); *My Book about*

Me by Dr. Seuss & Roy McKie (Random House); and *My Family, Myself* by Carol Batchelor (Hayes).

Helping our children develop healthy self-images cannot be accomplished in a summer or even in a year; it's a continual process of helping our children see themselves as God sees them. But as you apply some of these projects each summer, it is with the prayer that by summer's end your children's conclusions to "I am . . ." will be, "I am a child of God. I am happy. I am learning!"

CHAPTER 7

Plans for Producing

When we think of summer plans for our children, we often think of ways to keep them entertained. We wholeheartedly believe that your plans for the summer should include good times together with your children and things that are just good fun (we devoted two chapters to this), but we don't want you to become their social secretaries or personal maids!

We've just looked at ways you can use this summer to build your children's self-esteem. Let's continue with this thought and talk about how you can improve their self-image this summer by helping them develop competence and responsibility. We've planned for pleasure; now let's plan for production!

Helping your children plan and set goals so that by summer's end they can actually see progress, is a big help to their self-esteem. When they see they have accomplished something, it helps them feel good about themselves.

"I LOVE MYSELF!"

A friend of ours was in the process of teaching her young child to read. She was tucking Johnny in bed after he had just read his first book. She kissed him good-night and said, "I love you!"

Johnny smiled and said, "I do too!—I love you, Mommy, and I love myself!"

By helping your children with self-improvement this summer, you can help them say, "I love myself!"

PLANS FOR DEVELOPING COMPETENCE

In what areas would you like to help your children develop competence this summer? Is there a subject in school that needs extra attention? How's their letter-writing ability? Perhaps they've never discovered the joy of getting mail (the catch is they must write first!). Any gourmet-to-be cooks at your house? Maybe it's household skills you'd like to teach them—like how to use the washing machine, wax furniture, clean the toilet (can we call that a skill?), or polish silver. What about library skills, learning to ride a bike, learning the ABCs, or sewing on a button? The list of possibilities is endless.

A Skill a Week

Make your own list and plan to teach your children several skills during the summer. This could easily be incorporated into Children's Day or "Just-Me-and-Mom" times or a few minutes on Saturday morning. One super-organized mother made a list and decided to teach her child a skill a week. To make it realistic, she chose simple but valuable skills that did not require a large block of time to teach—like how to run the vacuum cleaner and change the bags, or how to load the dishwasher. Many times we do jobs ourselves instead of letting our children "help" because it's just less of a hassle to do it ourselves than to go back and switch the cups and glasses in the dishwasher to their proper places (or rewash and dry the dishes if your dishwasher has a human motor!).

A little time this summer invested in teaching your children "how tos" can prevent hours of frustration and allow the children to be a real help.

Seventy-Five Cents a Book

Want to encourage your child in reading, neatness, and spelling? Here's an idea from the Arps.

"One summer I incorporated into the boys' goals some activities that would give them an advantage when school started again. Joel was an okay student, but neatness and spelling were definitely not his strong suits. So I designed a reading program to help him improve these skills. He likes to read, so I selected a group of books from which he could choose. For each book that Joel read, wrote a report on (neatly), and learned to spell the misspelled words, I gave him seventy-five cents. If he finished ten books he would get an extra five dollars.

"I wish I could tell you he finished all ten books, but actually it was several less. But even though he didn't reach his original goal, Joel felt good about himself, for he accomplished much more than if we had not taken the time to set a goal. And when the new school year started, we observed improvement in his neatness and spelling. Also, there was an increased interest in reading."

Mailbox Surprises

Mom's proverb: "In order to receive a letter, one must first write a letter!" All children love to receive letters, especially those written only to them. Lucky is the child whose grandmother writes him/her letters— even when he/she never answers. What can you do this summer to encourage your children in the letter-writing department? Perhaps you have a budding author-to-be at your house. With just a little inspiration, a pencil, stationery, and encouragement, who knows what might happen?

One idea is to have a letter-writing session. Keep this in mind for a rainy Children's Day activity or a "Just-Me-and-Mom" time or whenever you have a free hour or so. Included could be catching up on correspondence and thank-yous and sending birthday and get-well cards. Make a list of all summer birthdays of family and friends and have a Children's Day activity of making birthday cards. You could cut out pictures and verses from old cards and magazines or make up your own verses and draw your own pictures. Then address the envelopes and write the date to be mailed in the corner where the stamp will go. As the summer progresses, mail them on the appropriate days.

Now for the mechanics of writing a letter: Choose a friend, grandparent, cousin, aunt, or pen pal to whom your child would like to write. It is best to have some children's stationery (lined, if possible) on hand. Otherwise, make your own with lined paper and stickers. Teach your child where to write the date, greeting, and so forth. Discuss what information can go into the letter—what has your child been doing, reading, or thinking about? What is he going to do tomorrow and next week? Anything to say "thank you" for? This might be a good opportunity to teach dictionary skills for words that are hard to spell.

Note: We have found if we write letters at the same time our children do, they are much more willing to keep at it.

Let younger children write their letters verbally. Mom writes down exactly what they say and then lets the child copy. This cuts down on the frustration for the child (and for Mom too) in having to spell every word very, very s-l-o-w-l-y!

Perhaps the most fun part of writing letters is what the mail carrier brings in reply! This activity will also benefit your children in preparing for the next school year.

Send for Summertime Freebies

When your children run out of people to write, send away for free information. This is a constructive and fun project, and they will love getting mail back—especially if they are patient. It usually takes four to six weeks for a reply, so perhaps this would be a fun early summer project.

For an up-to-date list of "freebies," we suggest the book *Free Stuff for Kids* published yearly by Meadowbrook. Check your local bookstore for other frccbic books.

Watch magazines for other free offers.

Hot Dogs à la Gourmet

One summer the Dillow girls learned a lot about cooking by preparing a meal each week. They started with simple meals—hot dogs and hamburgers—and by summer's end they were making spaghetti and tuna casserole. Here are some of their favorite recipes.

PIZZA MUFFINS

margarine	knife
1 pkg. English muffins, split in half	broiler or toaster oven
1 8-oz. can tomato sauce	cookie sheet
1/2 lb. ground beef	frying pan
1 4-oz. can mushrooms	wooden spoon
2 Tbsp. minced onions	can opener
1 tsp. oregano	
1/2 tsp. garlic salt	
1 pkg. sliced mozzarella cheese	

Lightly toast buttered muffin halves on cookie sheet under broiler. In frying pan, brown meat and pour off grease. Add mushrooms, sauce, onions, and seasoning. Let cook down until it is "sloppy joe" consistency. Put heaping spoonful on each muffin half. Top with slice of cheese and run under the broiler for one minute. Watch carefully. Makes 8 small pizzas.

Variations: Use chopped ham, bologna, or pepperoni in place of ground beef.

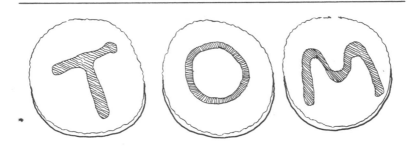

BRANDED PANCAKES

Make pancakes as directed on Bisquick package. Let batter trickle from teaspoon onto hot griddle to form a letter. Letters must be made backwards to be right when pancakes are served. Draw your initial backwards on a piece of paper for a pattern before you start.

When bottom side of initial has lightly browned, pour a regular spoonful of batter over initial.

Bake until bubbles appear, then turn and finish cooking.

Serve hot with butter and warm syrup or jelly.

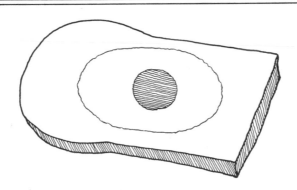

EGGS IN A FRAME

Pull center from a slice of bread, or cut out center with biscuit cutter.

Butter bread generously on both sides.

Brown bread "frames" on one side in moderately hot buttered frying pan. Turn over. Drop egg into center.

Cook slowly until egg white is set. (Cover pan until white starts to set.)

Sprinkle lightly with salt.

Lift out with pancake turner.

The above recipes are from Betty Crocker's *Cook Book for Boys & Girls,* pages 66 and 88.

TUNA DELIGHT

1 can tuna fish
1 can mushroom soup
1/4 cup milk

potato chips (about 3/4 of a medium-sized package)

Preheat oven at 325°.

Put some potato chips into a bowl. Break them into small pieces by pressing them against the bowl.

Empty a can of tuna fish into another bowl. Break up the pieces.

Put the potato chips into the bowl with the tuna fish. Add the mushroom soup and milk. Mix everything together.

Rub butter or margarine around the inside of a baking dish.

Pour the tuna fish mixture into the baking dish. Bake in the hot oven for 30 minutes.

A Pail of Patience

Children are growing up in a very sports-centered world. Along with beauty and brains, brawn and muscles are at the top of the world's system of values. If your child isn't cut out for being the star quarterback, what can you do to help him or her feel competent in the world of sports?

We believe there is a real benefit in helping our children do well in one summer sport and one winter sport. What's your child's forte? Swimming? Long-distance running? Soccer? Gymnastics?

When the Arp boys were young, they worked on learning to play a good game of tennis. This required that Claudia spend many hours working with them on the tennis courts. It took buckets of tennis balls and pails of patience, but she received tons of satisfaction as Jarrett, Joel, and Jonathan saw real improvement and felt a sense of accomplishment. Yes, it took a lot of Claudia's time, but there is no short cut. Sanity in the summer requires time, but the benefits are worth every second spent!

Perhaps you're thinking, *That's great for Linda and Claudia, but I'm just not "sporty" and can't teach my children.* Let us assure you that it is never too late. We both learned to play tennis and to ski after age thirty, and so can you!

PLANS FOR DEVELOPING RESPONSIBILITY

At this point you may be saying, "Yes, that would be wonderful to take the time for summer projects, but you don't know all the extra work I have in the summer. My 'nimble five-ring circus' is home with all the wet towels and three changes of clothes daily; and it's a known fact that carpets need vacuuming more often. In the summertime all the neighborhood kids think our house is the clubhouse! One hour after I clean the bathroom, there are three more dirty towels and an unflushed toilet. How can I keep my sanity, much less teach skills and tennis?"

Or maybe you are a single mom and you would like to be home with wet towels, unflushed toilets, and summer traffic—but it's just not a possibility! If you do work outside the home, you will need to find small blocks of time when you are home—such as Tuesday evening after supper or Saturday morning from nine to nine-thirty.

We believe there is real hope! Why not channel some of that untapped energy into making housekeeping a family affair?

Housekeeping—A Family Affair

Many different tactics have been used to motivate children to help around the house, and most don't work. Not the least among them are charts. If you're like us, you've already tried many, but we would like to share with you a couple of chart ideas that have actually worked. The key is variety and creativity. Don't expect one chart to motivate your child forever, but if it helps for a while—like a summer—it is worth considering!

One-Time Charts

If you're a skeptic, maybe you'll be willing to try our one-time check list. This is good to use when the children are bored or when you're trying to get through your household duties so you can begin a Children's Day activity. Make a list of jobs for each child and explain that when they finish there will be a little surprise for them. (This can be something to eat or an inexpensive toy.) Write out the check list on an index card like this:

```
          I Love Mom ✔
_____ Make up my bed
_____ Clean under bed
_____ Straighten my drawers
_____ Desk top neat
_____ Empty trash
_____ Fold clothes for Mom
_____ Empty dishwasher
_____ Read one chapter in Bible
          When finished bring to Mom for surprise!
```

Weekly Charts

At the Dillow house, Joy, Robin, and Tommy had weekly charts. We're including one of Joy's charts at age eleven (page 86). Joy's allowance was set at a certain amount. For each job that was done, she got a smiley face on the chart. Also, if all jobs were done well and cheerfully, the full allowance was received. For each job left undone, Joy got a check, and five cents was deleted for each check mark. The idea came about when Tasha, the Dillow's dog, joined the family. The children *promised* they would *totally* take care of her! In response to that plan, Linda's mother had quipped, "Every child needs a dog for his mother to take care of!" Linda *definitely* did not want this to become a reality, so the chart system was born.

Rules:
1. Every time I complete a job, I get a smiley face.
2. Every time I don't do a job, I get a check mark and I have to do the job anyway.
3. At the end of the week the check marks are added up and five cents is taken off for each check mark.
4. Any job done with a bad attitude will result in one check mark.
5. Room must be cleaned before I leave for school.

Apple-Picking Time

Charts can be for a one-time shot like the "I Love Mom" check list or weekly, as at the Dillow house. Another idea is to use a chart idea for a certain period of time, with a starting and an ending date.

JOBS FOR JOY

	Sat.	Sun.	Mon.	Tues.	Wed.	Thur.	Fri.
Make bed							
Clean room							
Clean hamster cage—Monday							
Special job							
Clean my dresser							
Brush my teeth twice daily							
Read one chapter in Bible each day							
Pick up "Tasha's Treasures"—Monday							
Feed Tasha 4 times a week—Sun., Tues., Thur., Sat.							
Clean my part of bookshelf							
Lay out clothes and bus ticket before going to bed							
Brush Tasha—Wed., Fri.							
Dust my part of room—Sun.							

The Arps used this approach when Claudia enrolled in a ten-week course. The need for little helpers around the house increased, so the following plan was devised. On a chart Claudia made a green felt apple tree and four fruit baskets and gave the red felt apples numbers that corresponded with specific jobs. The jobs were listed by the side of the apple tree. For instance:

1. Set the table, if you're able.
2. The bathroom I'll clean once this week to show you that I'm really sweet!

Fruit-picking time was Sunday evening, and the boys (her husband, Dave, participated too!) chose the jobs they wanted to do to help Claudia for the next week. Each week they chose new jobs.

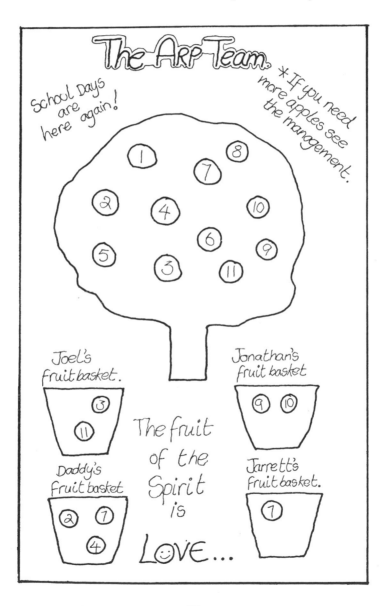

"I wish I could say it worked well for all ten weeks," she remembered. "It too got 'old,' but for the few weeks it lasted, the boys were a real help. It was definitely worth the time it took to make the chart."

SUMMER MONEY EARNERS

Another way to teach responsibility is to help our children earn some of their spending money. Good baby-sitters are hard to find, and perhaps your older children are growing into baby-sitting age and could use some summer training in the art of being a good baby-sitter.

Why not have a brain storming session with your children and list together ideas for summer jobs. One family did this and following are some of the things they wrote on their list—

1. Have a yard sale.
2. Grow tomatos and cucumbers and sell to neighbors. (They said to forget zucchini. Everyone has plenty.)
3. Do yard work (mow, pull weeds, plant flowers).
4. Water yards and plants on a regular basis for neighbors.
5. Teach younger children a sport—soccer, tennis, basketball.
6. Provide the entertainment for birthday parties.
7. Deliver balloons for special occasions.

For more suggestions see: *Extra Cash for Kids* by Larry Belliston and Kent Hank (Wolgemuth & Hyatt). This book contains one hundred moneymaking ideas and details on how to do the job, set prices, and avoid problems.

The Arp Peanut Brothers

The Arp boys developed two businesses. In the fall they helped earn their skiing money by making and selling wax Christmas tree decorations. In the summer (and throughout the year) they made and sold 100 percent pure homemade peanut butter. They kept books and records of things like time spent and jars sold, and each month they received their share of the profits.

This business venture proved to be an excellent way for them to develop responsibility and to see the benefits of hard work. One month one of the boys earned only fifteen cents while his brothers earned twelve dollars and five dollars. The next month he really got with it and did his share of the work and earned his share of the profits!

The Dillow Kinder-Gym Experience

For several summers the Dillow kids ran a kinder-gym. This summer job enabled them to earn money and learn skills. It also helped the mothers of young children in Vienna who had no day camps, mother's day outs, or other marvelous American inventions.

What is a kinder-gym? It's a combination kindergarten, gymnastics class, and baby-sitting service for three- to five-year-olds (or older). What do you do at a kinder-gym? Whatever keeps the children entertained and busy, which might include crafts, hikes, cooking, simple gymnastics skills, and lots of fun for the three-to-five set. (You may need to check with a local daycare licensing bureau to determine state regulations on such ventures.)

The Dillow gang pulled off kinder-gym three mornings a week from 9–12 A.M. The location was the Dillows' house and yard. (Yes, the house got messy each time.) To organize their new adventure, Joy, Robin, Tommy, and Niki sent out a letter to families they knew with young children, inviting them to sign up for the kinder-gym.

What did they learn through this experience? First, it's not easy to entertain three- to five-year-olds for three hours. They also discovered that some preschoolers are very uncooperative! They came to appreciate the importance of preparation and got in the habit of making snacks the day before and having everything ready before the children arrived. By the way, the Dillows found that *Sanity in the Summertime* has lots of simple, creative ideas, and using this book brought back unique memories of their own family fun in summers gone by!

The main thing the Dillow gang learned can be summed up in one word—responsibility! What did Linda learn through this experience? She learned that her children learning responsibility was more important than a neat and quiet house. Joy, Robin, Tommy, and Niki were excited about the money; Linda was excited about what they were learning.

PICK YOUR MAJOR

Remember you can't do everything. The Arp boys didn't run a kinder-gym, and the Dillow children didn't get involved in the peanut butter business. But Joy went three times a week to gymnastics and became an able gymnast. Tommy pursued several sports, and Robin developed responsibility by keeping up with her daily time of practicing the piano. None of the Arp boys pursued music. We decided no one family (or Super Mom) can try to do everything! Don't feel guilty if your children can't turn back flips or make peanut butter. Instead, *pick your major!*

Take an inventory in your family. What are your special interests? Choose the best way for *you* to help your children develop competence and responsibility this summer.

CHAPTER 8

Challenge Your Children

It is often said that children are a challenge. We would like to turn that around and say, "This summer, *challenge your children!*" In the previous chapter we discussed ideas for developing competence and responsibility in your children, incorporating these ideas into "Children's Day" and "Just-Me-and-Mom" times. Another suggestion for making these objectives become a reality in your children's lives this summer is to give them a Super Summer Challenge!

SUPER SUMMER CHALLENGE

Gail, a friend of ours, challenged her ten- and eleven-year-olds with a Super Summer Schedule. The purpose was to help them develop competence and responsibility in the following areas:

1. Spiritual
2. Physical
3. Home
4. Creative
5. Musical
6. Mental
7. Miscellaneous

The challenge was for eight weeks, and the object was to earn as many points as possible. Each point was worth twenty-five cents.

SUPER SUMMER SCHEDULE[1]

SCOTT Age 11	POINTS	SHANNON Age 10
SPIRITUAL		**SPIRITUAL**
Read Bible daily (Mark, Psalm 119). Write favorite verse in each chapter; illustrate one event. Write down everything about the Word of God in Psalm 119.	1	Read Bible daily (Mark, Psalm 119). Write favorite verse in each chapter; illustrate one event. Write down everything about the Word of God in Psalm 119.
Read one missionary biography.	10*	Read one missionary biography.
PHYSICAL		**PHYSICAL**
Run 1 mile in less than 8 minutes.	20	Run 1 mile.
Work up to 8 pull-ups.	10	Do flexed arm hang for 90 seconds.
Work up to 85 sit-ups in 2 minutes.	15	Work up to 85 sit-ups in 2 minutes.
HOME		**HOME**
Clean up room.	1	Clean up room.
Plan and cook an entire meal and clean up afterwards.	5	Plan and cook an entire meal and clean up afterwards.
Vacuum house.	2	Vacuum house.
CREATIVE		**CREATIVE**
Help build a house for Patches [rabbit].	10	Help build a house for Patches.
Help build and sand stool for Mom.	8	Sew an apron for Mom.
Design and make a useful Christmas present for someone.	4	Design and make a useful Christmas present for someone.
MUSICAL		**MUSICAL**
Learn a new song on the piano.	3*	Learn a new song on the piano.
Learn to play a hymn on the piano.	5	Learn to play a hymn on the piano.
MENTAL		**MENTAL**
Read a book and tell the plot to the family.	5*	Read a book and tell the plot to the family.
Work math review sheets.	1	Work math review sheets.

Write a letter using neat cursive and correct spelling.	1	Write a letter using neat cursive and correct spelling.

MISCELLANEOUS		MISCELLANEOUS
Help at garage sale.	1	Help at garage sale.
Wash car.	2	Wash car.

Rules:

1. You must work at least 1 hour per day on the projects. 1 point = 25 cents.

2. Items marked with an asterisk (*) require prior approval from Mom or Dad.

3. All work must be inspected and approved by Mom or Dad.

4. Many projects may be done repeatedly for additional points.

REMEMBER: THE MOST IMPORTANT QUALITY IS FAITHFULNESS DAY BY DAY!

This idea could be adjusted and used for various age groups. Or perhaps instead of picking seven areas, you might choose to work on three or four—or even one!

TEENAGE CHALLENGE

We asked a good friend who has older teenage children her suggestions for the teenage years. Her reply was, "Pray! Pray! Pray!" There is something about adolescence that causes feelings of incompetence in mothers!

Claudia remembers feeling inadequate as mother of a soon-to-be teen the spring before Jarrett's thirteenth birthday, and she had slipped off to a coffee shop to pray for herself and for Jarrett. She wrote a letter to Jarrett expressing her feelings. Perhaps you can relate to parts of it.

Dear Jarrett,
You're soon to enter "teenagehood." What an exciting time of life. . . . You're entering an age when friends are so important—that's fine—just remember mothers are important too! Mothers love to hear the words, "Mom, guess what happened at school today!" . . . Jarrett, please let me still be on your team—I was a teenager once. . . . How I wish I had talked more, shared more openly with my parents—guess I was too shy. May I be to you a sounding board to express your real feelings, fears, joys, and struggles. I pledge to you to keep our conversations *just between us*—locked in my heart to pull out someday and trea-

sure. I've never been a mother of a teenager before—I know I'll make a lot of mistakes! I'm human, you know. Will you help me to keep our relationship a healthy, loving, growing (but not a smothering) one? Can we both use the words, "I'm sorry; please forgive me" often?

Soon after writing the letter to Jarrett, Claudia received a letter from our friend Phyllis with the following suggestion for mothers entering "the teenage years."

For Paul's thirteenth birthday we gave him these challenges: Memorize Philippians 2:3–11, run a mile in under eight minutes, earn forty dollars from the sale of handmade items (he made fifty dollars), and do a report on Albert Schweitzer (it was excellent!). He made them all and it was a fun way to enter teenagehood. Thought you might be interested for Jarrett!

The Arps thought this was an excellent idea, so they adapted it for Jarrett the summer before he became a teenager. If you already have a teenager, why not give him/her a fourteenth Birthday Challenge . . . or fifteenth or sixteenth . . . ?

Think through the different areas of your teen's or preteen's life and decide on the challenges that would help strengthen and encourage him/her. These would be different for each child as he/she reaches teenagehood and can be uniquely designed to help where help is most needed. The Arps divided Jarrett's Teenage Challenge into four areas:

1. Physical goals
2. Spiritual goals
3. Intellectual goals
4. Practical goals

Here is Jarrett's Teenage Challenge. Maybe it will challenge you to challenge your soon-to-be teen!

Physical Goals

1. Swim 100 meters and earn your Boy Scout Swimming Skill Award.

2. Run a mile in under 8 minutes. (He did it in 7 minutes, 25 seconds!)

Spiritual Goals

1. Complete Bible study of Proverbs—"Traps to Avoid."

2. Complete a "Code of Conduct" Bible study and work out your

own code of conduct for your teenage years. Includes topical Bible study of the following areas:

    A. Obedience—Disobedience
    B. Respect—Disrespect
    C. Honesty—Dishonesty
    D. Responsibility—Irresponsibility
    E. Spirit of Rejoicing—Moodiness/Grumpiness

We are including these Bible studies at the end of the book in Appendix I for your use. Or you may work out your own or use other resource material.

Intellectual Goals

1. Review math.
2. Read biography of a present-day missionary and give an oral report to our family and one other family.

Practical Goals

1. Plan and execute an overnight campout with Dad. (This proved to be an excellent time for father and son!)
2. Earn thirty dollars. What you earn and save will be matched!
3. Work out a budget for fall.

Jarrett accepted this challenge and really worked hard. He completed it by his birthday and received a reward (a new camera) and also a "Certificate of Teenagehood," which was framed and hung in his room. Months later, Jarrett commented that the Teenage Challenge had helped him grow spiritually and that it was good to know he had accomplished something.

Claudia reported a few months later: "We are now well into our journey through teenagehood. This road is not always bump free and I'm sure we will make some wrong turns, but I feel that Jarrett and I are enjoying our journey much more because of this time of preparation."

When Problems Arise

The week of Jarrett's thirteenth birthday, Claudia felt she had really found the answer to teenage problems. She *had* found a great tool—the Teenage Challenge—but tools are not an end in themselves. Rather, they are used to build, improve, and perfect.

More than once Claudia has been able to sit down and deal with problems and potential problems by retalking through the Teenage

Challenge Bible studies—letting the Holy Spirit do the convicting (instead of a legal parent prosecutor!).

What we are trying to say is that when hard areas arise—and they will—it is possible to deal with them by looking once again at the commitments your teen made as a result of the Teenage Challenge. To deal with the problem through restudying God's Word is one way of building your relationships with your teenagers and not tearing them down through tears and accusations.

Whether you have teens or tots, we challenge you to challenge your children this summer!

(For more information about how to develop your own teenage challenge and to prepare for the teenage years, we suggest you read Claudia's book—*Almost 13*.)

CHAPTER 9

Putting Sonshine in Your Summer

How can you help your children "shine for Jesus" this summer? One three-year-old's interpretation was to strip and generously spread baby powder and baby oil all over her cute, chubby body! How wonderful it would be if making our children shine with godly qualities this summer were so simple! Just sprinkle them with powder three times a day and love, joy, peace, patience, kindness, goodness, faithfulness, gentleness, and self-control would result. But alas, it's not so simple.

In Deuteronomy 6:4–8 we read God's blueprint for producing godly qualities in our children's lives:

> Hear, O Israel! The LORD is our God, the LORD is one! And you shall love the LORD your God with all your heart and with all your soul and with all your might. And these words, which I am commanding you today, shall be on your heart; and you shall teach them diligently to your sons and shall talk of them when you sit in your house and when you walk by the way and when you lie down and when you rise up. And you shall bind them as a sign on your hand and they shall be as frontals on your forehead.

In these verses we see three ways that we are to teach our children:

1. informal teaching
2. formal education
3. modeling

Remember that one of our goals for the summer is to help our children grow spiritually. So let's see how we can use these three methods with our children this summer.

INFORMAL TEACHING

We are to talk to our children about God's love and His law as we sit in our house, walk by the way, lie down, and rise up.

"I remember vividly one night years ago," Linda recalls. "Jody was traveling and it had been a *long* day. 'Exhaustion' is not a strong enough word to describe how I felt. I filled the bathtub, added bath oil, and settled in for a luxurious, lengthy soak. Oh, how good it felt! I was alone at last! Then three little knocks on the bathroom door told me I was not as alone as I thought.

"'Who is it?'

"Four-year-old Robin answered, and I immediately told her to go back to bed!

"'But Mommy!' the little voice continued. 'I want to ask Jesus into my heart. . . .'"

Children's questions often seem to come at the most inconvenient times—ten minutes before guests are arriving for dinner, when we have a list of important things to do, or when we're tired and longing to stumble to bed. God instructs us to talk about His truths in the midst of the everyday joys and struggles of life. Often it only takes five or ten minutes to meet the need of a child's heart and relate the situation to God, but how difficult it is to stop our schedules and be available!

One family told of the discussion they had at the dinner table. The oldest daughter began, "Guess what? I got to show a new girl around school today. She's nice, but she sure has problems. The reason she had to move is that her mom can't keep her any longer and she doesn't even know why. She has to live with her dad and stepmother. She sure is mixed up about it."

This conversation gave the parents the chance to explain, once again, God's ideal for marriage—one man and one woman for life. They asked such questions as, "How do you think your friend feels?" "How would you feel?" "How can you show your new friend special love?" All the children got involved in caring about someone else's needs.

Be a Sitting Mom

Perhaps mealtime is the only time you sit. Yet we're commanded to talk to our children as we sit in our house! Think for a moment . . . when was the last time you tried sitting in your house? You sit in the car, in the dentist's chair, and in waiting rooms, but what about in your house? (Sitting in front of the TV doesn't count!)

The summertime offers many opportunities to do just that—to sit with your children on a hot day with a glass of cool lemonade. If you're like us, though, the tendency might be to say, "Children, here is some cool lemonade and cookies. How about a snack? Just remember to eat in the kitchen and don't spill anything!" Then we hurry on to the washing, the letter writing, the creative project, or the important phone call that just can't wait, feeling really good inside that our cookies were home-made. But maybe even more than our thoughtful snack, our children need a "sitting mom." (Besides, we could use the rest!)

Claudia relates, "One afternoon the boys came in to 'refuel.' That day I took the time to sit down with them to talk, and before long I was really absorbed in the conversation and forgot completely about the other jobs desperately waiting to be done. From football to butterflies to Popeye to burns—the subjects jumped like a kangaroo. And again I saw the tremendous opportunity to relate our everyday happenings to our heavenly Father.

"Jonathan and I talked about how God had changed the 'worm' into a beautiful butterfly and how this is a picture of how God changes us when we become Christians. Joel's burnt finger was hurting, and we talked about how nice it would be if pain didn't exist. But then we decided God was very wise in allowing the sensation of pain because if Joel had not felt any pain when he touched the stove, he could have been badly burned. What does it take? A few moments to relate things back to God and demonstrate that our Christianity is not just a Sunday affair but encompasses the totality of life."

Summer Strategies for Sonshine

Each summer week is filled with opportunities to teach informally. The following is a sampling of lessons we discovered.

1. A quarrel with a friend caused anger, hurt, and bitterness in one child. This provided the opportunity for a wonderful talk together on forgiveness and doing what 1 Peter 3:9 says to do—return a blessing for an insult.

2. Angry, unkind words between brothers—an occasion for reading Ephesians 4 together.

3. A "too-short" haircut produced tears, sobs, and threats that she would hide until it grew out! A perfect time to share how God works "all things" (even "too-short" hair) together for good in our lives (Rom. 8:28).

4. A summer walk amid beautiful flowers, towering trees, and a blue sky was an opportunity to remember together the good things God has given us to enjoy.

We learn to be more sensitive to informal teaching opportunities when we:

1. Talk about times during the past few weeks when we used an opportunity to comment on God's greatness, His love, or some Bible truth with the children.

2. Try to remember situations when we missed a chance to relate an everyday happening to God's love and His presence.

3. Count the times that we spent time with each child alone, talking and sharing needs and concerns.

4. Think specifically about *today*. Which opportunities did we use? Which ones did we miss?

We encourage you to ask yourself these four questions each week this summer and to determine to be more sensitive to the many opportunities for informal teaching that are right before your eyes. The most important teaching takes place when the "need" is there, and in the hot, humid days of summer many needs will be present in your children's lives. They are all opportunities to let the "Sonshine" in.

FORMAL TEACHING

Deuteronomy 6 also instructs us to teach the love and law of God *diligently* to our sons and daughters. What picture does the word *diligently* bring to your mind?

Roget's Thesaurus lists synonyms of diligent: "hardworking," "industrious," "unrelenting." Diligent teaching implies that we are to have definite plans for communicating God's teachings to our children. They need to see that we value God's Word enough to share it with them regularly.

Without fail, each evening after dinner Mr. and Mrs. Jones read a chapter from the Bible. They're in Numbers now, and the number of interested Joneses is almost nil. It's a "sit-still-and-soon-the-pain-will-be-over" atmosphere as another family attempts to reach and train their children. It could be that the one thing the children are learning is that when they have families, "family devotions" will be out! Is this the diligent formal training that Deuteronomy 6 speaks about?

Our two families have read through books of the Bible, a chapter each day, but anything done the same way every day can become monotonous. Perhaps one of the most important things to remember as you plan summertime devotions is to gear them to the children's age levels, interests, and needs. There are scores of wonderful teaching aids available today for every age group.

Preschoolers (2–5 Years and Older)

Here are some books that children love:

1. *The Bible in Pictures for Little Eyes* by Kenneth Taylor (Tyndale).
2. *The Muffin Family* series (Harvest House).
3. All the Arch Books (Concordia).
4. *He Is My Shepherd* by David and Helen Haidle (Multnomah).
5. *Little Visits with God* by Jahsmann and Simon (Concordia).

Video: *One-Minute Bible Stories* by Shari Lewis (Sparrow).

Children's Day—Plants Grow and So Do I!

Because summertime is a time of planting and watching things grow, it can be a time for talking and learning about spiritual growth. During a Children's Day look up and perhaps write on a piece of paper one or all of the following verses: 1 Peter 2:2, Ephesians 4:15, 2 Peter 3:18, and 1 Thessalonians 3:12. Your child might enjoy drawing pictures to depict his/her understanding of these verses.

Activity:

Plant together bean seeds, radish seeds, or any fast-growing seeds. As you daily water and watch the seeds grow, you can continually talk together about how we grow in our Christian lives.

Here are several ideas for planting.

1. HANGING BASKETS

Materials needed:

Plastic berry basket; old pair pantyhose; potting soil; four pieces yarn, each twelve inches long; fast-growing seeds (green bean, lima bean, nasturtium, marigold, radish, tomato, carrot); scissors; and bucket to mix soil.

How to plant:

Cut rectangular piece from top of pantyhose. Line the basket. Tie one piece of yarn to top corners of basket. Knot the four pieces together at top to hang level. Fill basket one-half to three-fourths full of moistened potting soil. Plant seeds just under soil surface. (If you soak seeds in warm water overnight before planting, they will sprout in three to four days.) Hang basket outside in a tree. Water now and every day.

2. EGGSHELL GARDEN

Materials needed:

Eggshell halves, seeds, potting soil, egg carton, container to mix soil, and Popsicle sticks.

How to plant:

Fill eggshell halves with moist potting soil. Set them in egg carton. Plant several seeds in each shell. Plant a variety of seeds or all the same type. Use Popsicle sticks to mark the different kinds of seeds. Place in a bright window. Keep just barely moist. To transplant outdoors, gently crush eggshells and plant the entire thing.

School Age (Ages 6–12 and Older)

Some suggested books to read to the children and to encourage them to read themselves are:

1. Their own *The Living Bible.*
2. *Stories for the Children's Hour* by Kenneth Taylor (Moody).
3. *Devotions for the Children's Hour* by Kenneth Taylor (Moody).

4. *Treasures of the Snow* and other books by Patricia St. John.
5. *Alexi's Secret Mission* and other books by Anita Deyneka.
6. *Sugar Creek Gang* series by Paul Hutchens (Moody).
7. *The Sowers* series (Mott Media).
8. *The Guessing Books* by Fern Neal Stocker (Moody).
9. *The Student Bible* (NIV).
10. *The Picture Bible* (Zondervan).
11. *Beginners Bible* (Queststar).
12. *Bible Studies* by Paula Rinehart (NavPress).
    - *Never Too Small for God*
    - *One of a Kind*
    - *Stuck Like Glue*

Children's Day (Ages 6–12 and Older)

On this particular Children's Day teach the value of memorizing God's Word. The object is to have the children memorize two verses each week this summer.

Activity:

First choose the verses and write them on small cards—or better yet, have the children write them.

Craft:

Make a case for the memory cards so they can be taken on trips and learned well.

Materials needed:

felt in two or three colors
needle with a large eye
yarn in a pretty color

To make case:

Have the children cut two pieces of felt just a little bigger than the memory cards. Use the yarn and needle to stitch up three sides. Use the other colors of felt to cut out and paste designs on the case. Let the children create!

"Just-Me-and-Mom" Sonshine Time
(Ages 8–12 and Older)

For the month of July (or any month) help your child make a Proverbs notebook.

Materials needed:
five-by-seven spiral notebook or any size
pen or pencil
stickers, if desired, to decorate the pages
colored pencils

We selected July because there are thirty-one chapters in Proverbs and thirty-one days in July, so make thirty-one pages with the date and chapter to be read that day. Your child's summer devotions project will be:

1. To read one chapter of Proverbs each day.
2. To write down in the notebook a favorite verse from the chapter.
3. To draw a picture with the colored pencils about something in that chapter (optional).
4. To share the Proverbs notebook with you once a week or each day.

One of our main goals as mothers should be to teach our children to learn independently from God's Word. This Proverbs notebook is a short-term project that can start them on their way.

Build a Castle

Many learning times are planned at home, but don't fail to take advantage of all the opportunities that trips and travel afford during the summer. On your next visit to the beach, take time to read together the story about the houses built on sand and on rock (Matt. 7:24–27). When the tide is out, build a sand castle below the high-tide line. Beside your sand castle pile a few heavy rocks. Then watch what happens when the tide comes in. Share ideas on how this illustrates Jesus' story. Help your children identify Jesus as the "Rock." Let them know that you trust Him because He is dependable and a safe foundation for life.

Sing Praises

While traveling in your car, sing songs of praise together and read from a book. One summer the traveling Dillows decided to read *Alexi's Secret Mission* as they journeyed from Oregon to Rhode Island by car.

The only problem was that the children were so interested in the story that it was finished before they had driven out of Oregon, and another book had to be found for the remainder of the long trip.

Order Other Resources Today

Focus on the Family offers many wonderful family resources including the following magazines:

1. *Clubhouse* (8–12 yrs)
2. *Clubhouse, Jr.* (7 and under)
3. *Promise* (girls 12 & older)
4. *Breakaway* (boys 12 & older)
5. Don't overlook excellent family videos like *McGee and Me* Bible videos.

MODELING

Thus far we have seen how Deuteronomy 6 instructs us as parents to teach and train our children informally and formally. The passage would make us feel better if it were *only* directed toward our children and not toward us! But God says the first and most important thing is that *we* are to love the Lord our God with all *our* hearts and souls. We can't build into our children what is not real in our own lives.

Children are experts at detecting fakes! One little girl asked her mother, "Why do I have to pray every night? You don't ever pray."

A young boy questioned his father, "Daddy, is the Bible really God's book?"

Piously the father replied, "Oh yes, son. This is God's book."

"Well, Daddy," the boy replied, "we ought to give it back to God then, because we never use it here."

Wobbly Models

We are overwhelmed by the fact that we can take our children no further in their relationships with God than we've come ourselves. Our children would not call us hypocrites, but they're *very* aware that often we're "wobbly models"!

"Hearing the children screaming at one another," Linda recalls, "I stormed into the room, shouting, 'Would you stop screaming at one another! That's not the way to handle the problem!'

"Their puzzled looks conveyed the convicting truth that Mother was handling the problem by *yelling*—just what I'd told them not to do. The model had wobbled and was about to fall over. I looked at the children and said, 'Mommy blew it, kids. I just did the very thing I asked you not to do. Will you please forgive me? Let's all start over again and handle it right.'"

Teaching by example may seem to be an impossible task. However, God does not ask us to be perfect models. Larry Richards says it well:

> I am never to communicate perfection to my children or even to attempt to! The Bible says that we all sin, and that failure to recognize and admit sins, and confess them to the Lord breaks our fellowship with Him. The same passage suggests that we are to live with others just as we live with God—openly, honestly, confessing, relying on forgiveness and loving to maintain relationships (see Eph. 4:25–32). So, we can be effective Christian parents *If we are growing Christians,* and if we let our children see us, not as perfect, but as *seeking to grow.*[1]

Our children learn how to handle failure, mistakes, and sin by watching us deal with them. It is exciting for us to see how our children are quick to ask us for forgiveness. Where did they learn to humble themselves and ask forgiveness? From us—we had to ask them for forgiveness when we yelled, convicted without a trial, didn't try to understand, and so on and so on. You get the point: We can be good models *if* we have a relationship with God through Christ and are seeking to grow in Him.

Planting Comes before Growing

That last sentence said *if.* The starting point of being a good model to our children and teaching them the love of God is for us to love the Lord with all our hearts. We can't be seeking to grow as Christians unless a relationship with Christ has been established.

Living in America, most of us have heard all our lives that God loves us (John 3:16) and that we are selfish and sinful (Rom. 3:23; 6:23). We know that Christ died on a cross to forgive the sin of the world, but too often it's all head knowledge. Both of us lived more than twenty years knowing these things, but not knowing God. Sin to us was murder, adultery, and other gross deeds.

In individual ways we both learned at about the same time in our lives that sin is not just "deeds" but attitudes—an attitude of indifference towards God. This attitude of indifference can be active or passive. It can be doing and trying our best this summer without any reference to God. Christianity is not a religion, but a relationship with a living, personal God.

Perhaps the following illustration will help show how this relationship is established and how God's love and forgiveness can be experienced this summer.

Suppose you receive a speeding ticket and are summoned to appear in court. As you stand before the judge, you are declared guilty. The sentence is fifty dollars or five days. Meekly you begin to open your checkbook, but just then the judge stands up and takes off his robe. You see to your astonishment that it is your father. He comes toward you and says, "Honey, you're guilty. You've transgressed the law and you deserve to pay the penalty. But because I love you, I want to pay it for you." With that he pulls out *his* checkbook and writes a check for fifty dollars.

This is a picture of what God, our Father, did when Jesus died on the cross. God, the righteous judge, declared us guilty of sin. But as our loving Father, He did not want us to have to pay the penalty of eternal death and separation from Him, so He sent His only Son to die that we might be forgiven and have eternal life. When Jesus Christ cried His final words from the cross, "It is finished" (or literally from the Greek, "paid in full"), He was paying our penalty just as the judge did in the story.

Suppose the penalty had been paid by your father (the judge), but you still had to make a decision. Would you be a rebellious child and defiantly say, "Thanks, but no thanks. You can keep your check. I'll do it myself"? Or would you reach out and gratefully accept the gift offered in love?

In the same way each of us must decide what we will do with God's gift of forgiveness and eternal life. Our prayer is that if you are not certain whether you have received God's gift, you will reach out and accept it now.

How do you do that? By simply talking to God in prayer—admitting that you are sinful, thanking Him for dying to forgive your sin, and asking Him to come into your heart and life and begin to make you into the person He wants you to be.

Receiving Christ as our Savior and Lord is the first step toward being the teacher and model our children need. When the law and love of God is first in our hearts, we can then talk informally of Him, teach diligently about Him, and be a model (sometimes good, sometimes wobbly) of His love.

One of the goals for this summer is to help your children grow spiritually. You cannot in one summer instill all godly qualities like love, joy, peace, patience, kindness, goodness, faithfulness, gentleness, and self-control into your children's lives. Again we say, *pick your major!*

What does each child need most? Evaluate your children and plan to major on one spiritual area for each child. This means perhaps one child will do a Proverbs notebook, as she needs to develop a consistent Quiet Time. Another child will read three missionary biographies and write reports, as he needs his vision stretched. A third child will read through *The Bible Story Book* daily with Mommy, and so on. . . .

What do you want to see God do in your child's life this summer? Begin by bringing this request before God, and then determine to disciple your children and let the "Son" shine into their summer and yours.

CHAPTER 10

Sharing Your Sonshine

A friend wrote us that her summer plans with her children included plans for pleasure, plans to produce new skills and responsibility, and also plans to help her children learn to serve—to share their "Sonshine" with others. Her "action plan for service" worked. During summer vacation her fifteen-year-old daughter helped a young foreign child learn to read English, and her thirteen-year-old son took care of an elderly man's yard—not for money but to give of themselves and to show God's love.

Summer is a perfect time to help our children get out of their own world and view the needs and problems of others. Galatians 6:10 can become a reality in their lives: "So then, while we have opportunity, let us do good to all men, and especially to those who are of the household of the faith."

In our nation of plenty, too often our children's attitude is "what can I get?" instead of "what can I give?" A child who can walk and talk is old enough to begin learning to care about others. If the training begins then, it can carry over into the self-centered teenage years and throughout life. It's never too early or too late. So how do we begin?

There are four basic steps to be worked through to insure that our children are really being taught.

1. Pray.
2. Teach what the Scriptures say.
3. Be an example yourself (we can't get away from being models!).
4. Take them through the process.

You'll see how workable these four steps are as we relate them to planning for summer service.

1. *Pray*—"Commit your way to the LORD, / Trust also in Him, and He will do it" (Ps. 37:5).

   a. Choose from verses listed under step 2 and pray that they will become real in your children's lives.
   b. Thank God for healthy bodies, time, and energy with which to serve others.
   c. Ask God *specifically* to show you and your children
      • WHO to serve,
      • HOW to serve,
      • WHEN to serve.

2. *Teach your children what the Scriptures say* about serving others with our time, abilities, and money. The following verses deal with serving others.

Hebrews 13:16	Proverbs 25:21
Isaiah 58:10–11	Acts 20:35
Leviticus 19:32	Romans 12:10
John 15:12	Ephesians 4:32
Matthew 25:40	Philippians 2:3–4
Luke 3:10–11	Proverbs 22:9
Colossians 3:23–24	1 Timothy 6:18
James 2:15–17	Matthew 7:12
Galatians 6:10	John 13:34–35
1 John 3:18	2 Corinthians 9:7

Now that you have a long list of verses to use, here are some suggestions on ways to teach the Scriptures to children.

   a. For any age—Write the verses on slips of paper, put them in a container, and have your children draw one each day and read it to the family. Then discuss what the verses mean and what we can do this summer to fulfill God's commandments.
   b. For older children—Give each child a list of the Scriptures and a notebook. Ask him/her to look up each verse, write it in his notebook, and then write "what this verse means" and "what this verse means to me."

   Illustration: Hebrews 13:16—"And do not neglect doing good and sharing; for with such sacrifices God is pleased."

   "What does it mean?"—It means we're supposed to do nice

110

things for people and that God likes it when we do nice things and share.

"What does it mean to me?"—It means I should share my things with others and do good and nice things.

c. Stories for reading

For younger children, read the Arch Books: *The Rich Fool* or *The Boy Who Gave His Lunch Away*. Another good selection is Shari Lewis's *One-Minute Stories.*

For older children:
- Read Luke 10:25–37 (parable of the Good Samaritan). Ask: What does it say? What does it say to me?
- Read Mark 12:41–44 (parable of the widow's mite). Ask: What does it say? What does it say to me?
- Read together, or have your child read alone, a biography of Amy Carmichael. Have your child write a book review about "What I learned about sharing with others from Amy Carmichael."

3. *Be an example* of what you are teaching about sharing with others. Remember, the children are always watching!

4. *Take them through the process.* Begin by asking them for ideas of how they can serve others this summer. If you have studied some of the Scriptures together and talked about sharing their Sonshine with others, they should have lots of ideas. Help them decide which projects are suited to their ages, abilities, interests, and availability. Then walk through the projects with them.

Our friend whose fifteen-year-old daughter taught a foreign child to read did not just *suggest* it and then step out of the picture. She encouraged her daughter to go to the nearby elementary school and talk with the first-grade teacher about how she should teach the young child. The teacher gave her suggestions and books to use. The mother also continually checked with her daughter, and they talked weekly about the child's reading progress. The daughter did the weekly training, but the mother was involved in the process with her.

PICK YOUR MAJOR

To help you and your children enjoy your summertime creative sharing, some ideas are listed below for you to consider.

1. Visit a nursing home or retirement home.¹ Be sure to call ahead to find the best time to visit. Ask for names of people in the home who

would especially welcome visitors. Also ask if your family can bring treats and gifts to share. The children can make their favorite cookies or brownies, then pack them in small plastic bags tied with colorful ribbons. Perhaps they could include a verse in each bag: "I will be your God through all your lifetime, yes, even when your hair is white with age. I made you and I will care for you. I will carry you along and be your Savior" (Isa. 46:4, TLB).

This could be a wonderful way to spend a Children's Day. In the morning bake cookies and put them in plastic bags. Write verses on pieces of colored paper and enclose in bags. Tie a bright ribbon around each bag. In the afternoon visit the retirement or nursing home. The children can deliver their "goodies" and talk to the people, asking questions like, "Where were you born?" and "How long have you lived here?" They can also sing a song or read a story.

2. Ask your pastor for the names of lonely people in your church.

    a. Bake a treat and take it to the person, or
    b. Send a friendly card to say hello.

3. Offer to do errands for an elderly person in your neighborhood.

4. Bake cookies for a "Children's Day" activity. Send them to service personnel, college students, or anyone who needs cheering up.

5. Contact Child Evangelism (if available in your city) and plan a "Good News Club" with your children to reach out and share the message of Christ with their friends. When you think of sharing your Sonshine this summer, remember the best way to share is to tell others how they can know Christ personally. Child Evangelism can be an encouragement and help to you in reaching out.

6. Make a card and send it to an elderly relative or hospital patient (you can ask your pastor for names). Perhaps you could use a Children's Day or a "Just-Me-and-Mom" time to make several "Fabric and Yarn Cards" to send to lonely people.

Materials needed:
fabric scraps
yarn scraps
scissors
glue
construction paper
How to make: First cut the construction paper into a size that will fit in an envelope (or make a big card and mail it in a manila envelope). If desired, your child can first draw a design or picture on the card with a

pencil, then cut out fabric and yarn and paste it on the outline to make a beautiful fabric-and-yarn collage picture card.

7. Send a "cookie-dough gift" through the mail. Do you know a child in your town or another town who is confined indoors due to illness, or a child that just needs "extra caring"? These "send-a-dough cookies" are perfect! Your child makes the dough, packages it, and mails it. The receiver adds a few ingredients and—presto!—"Send-a-Cookies" are made!

SEND-A-COOKIES RECIPE

For two batches—you can send both or send one and keep one.

2½ cups flour
1 tsp. baking soda
1¼ tsp. salt
1 cup sugar
1 cup packed brown sugar

1½ cups shortening
3½ cups quick cooking oats
1 cup raisins
1 cup chocolate chips

Stir together the flour, soda, and salt; stir in sugars. Cut in the shortening until blended. Thoroughly stir in oats. Makes about 10 cups. Measure half of mix (about 5 cups) into plastic bag; add ½ cup chocolate chips and ½ cup of the raisins; close bag tightly. Put the remaining mix, raisins, and chocolate chips into another bag and close tightly.

To mail: Send it in a container where it can be sealed up well, like in a plastic sack, then a box. Include the following instructions on how to bake!

How to Bake: Empty one bag of the cookie mix into a bowl. With a wooden spoon, make a hole in the center. Into the hole drop one egg, 1/3 cup milk, 1/2 tsp. vanilla. With a spoon or fork mix the liquid ingredients into the dry ingredients (can use clean hands if necessary). Drop by teaspoons a few inches apart, on an un-greased cookie sheet. Bake in a preheated oven of 350° for 12 to 15 minutes. One bag of mix makes about 4 1/2 dozen cookies.

8. Grandmothers need loving, too! Why not use a Children's Day to make "Fingerprint Cards" and send one to Grandmother and another to an elderly woman in your town?

Materials needed:
sheets of white paper or construction paper cut to make a card
scissors
ink pad
color markers or crayons

How to make: After you have cut the paper in the shape card you want, have children press their fingers one at a time on the ink pad and then on their cards. Flowers, bees, and any number of designs and pictures can be created! The markers or crayons can be used to add stems to the flowers or wings to the bees!

9. Send a box to missionaries. Save money and buy or make special surprises for missionary friends or missionaries your church supports. If you're super-organized, you and the children can write a letter to the missionaries first (or call their agency), asking them what they need. If there is not time for a letter, here are some ideas that are always appreciated.

- Christian books, anything new and stimulating
- children's books (in many countries it is difficult to find books in English)
- Christian books for children

- Jell-O
- chocolate chips
- cake mixes
- salad dressing mixes
- spaghetti and sloppy joe mixes
- games and puzzles for children
- brown sugar

You can spend a Children's Day buying, wrapping, and mailing the package (it will take a whole day). Also, be prepared, as it costs a bit to mail overseas. Be sure to mail the "slow boat" way, as it is cheapest. It will take a couple of months for Europe and much longer for Asia, but what joy your love and thoughtfulness will bring when your special box arrives!

TODAY IS THE DAY

All the things we have suggested in this chapter are good ideas, but they will remain just that unless we put "feet" to them and make them happen! Today is a good day to begin to pray—for our children and for us—that we will know how to reach out and share our Sonshine with others. It's a good day to begin to teach what the Scriptures say about serving and sharing with others, to evaluate our own lives and see if we are an example of what we are teaching, and to be prepared to "walk through the process" with our children. Yes, it takes time. Yes, it is work. But it is also a joy and a privilege to share our Sonshine!

CHAPTER 11

Traveling Made Triumphant

What visions fill your mind when you think of summer traveling? One father said he felt condemned to drive his tribe across hundreds of hectic miles, filled with screams, attempted homicides, and innumerable unscheduled pit stops, as he wished the kids had taken more Dramamine and he had taken several extra Excedrin![1]

Unless you are in the minority, your summer plans will include at least one car, plane, or train trip with your children. Whether you head for grandparents, Disney World, or the unknown, you know there will be hours of real family closeness!

TRAVELING CAN BE FUN

Now we don't claim in any way, shape, or form to be "expert mothers." We learned, grew, and improved, but we're a long way from "expert." There is one area, however, in which we have had lots of experience—*traveling!* Each summer, many long days were spent in cars, trains, and planes as our children followed their parents on speaking tours. One summer the Dillow family logged well over one hundred hours of "family togetherness" in their VW van.

Our motto (which on some days even we doubted) was "Better to spend long days in the car than lonely days at home!" Our friends questioned our motto and disbelieved us when we said, "Traveling by car with three children *can* be *fun!*" Hectic fun, yes, and sometimes exasperating—but it was still fun! We could make this statement because we found a key to traveling sanity—*planning!*

Where Are We Going?

There is a song that asks, "Where are we going, what are we doing, what are we going to see?" Let's pretend we're taking a family vacation and try to answer these three questions.

"Where are we going?" Let's say we are traveling from Texas to California, and three to four days will be spent in the car each way. We will drive through Texas, New Mexico, Arizona, and part of California.

"What are we doing?" We plan to visit grandparents, take a trip to Disneyland, and spend several days at the ocean.

"What are we going to see?" Miles and miles of freeway, lots of desertlike terrain, maybe an Indian reservation, and if we're willing to drive the necessary out-of-the-way distance, the Grand Canyon.

Now that we have the necessary information, we can begin to plan.

Make a Travel Notebook

Have your children make travel notebooks, a great activity for elementary-school-age children. Buy a looseleaf notebook, dividers, and paper. The various sections of the notebook for our pretend trip will be:

1. *Interesting facts*—about Texas, New Mexico, Arizona, California, Indian reservations, or the Grand Canyon. Using an encyclopedia or library books, each child will write information on one of the above topics and share it with the family. This will help them all be better prepared for the trip.

One summer the Dillow children made travel notebooks before their family vacation. Two of the children copied word for word from *World Book,* but they were very proud of their "reports" as they read them one evening to the family.

2. *Travel Log Section*—here the child can write a brief daily diary of the trip.

3. *Postcard Section*—filled with blank, unlined paper ready for pasting interesting postcards gathered on the trip.

4. *Quiet Time Section*—where the child can record special verses or prayer requests each day.

5. *Money Section*—where the child can keep account of his/her own money and how it disappears!

6. *Blank Section*—blank sheets of paper for drawing, tic-tac-toe, or anything.

Why not plan a "Travel Notebook Children's Day" a few weeks before your summer trip? Spend the day:

1. Buying notebooks, dividers, paper, etc.

2. At the library or at home researching and writing down interesting facts.
3. Making notebook divisions and getting the "Summer Travel Notebook" ready to use.

Think ahead about your trip—where you will be traveling and what you will be doing. All of this helps you to plan. But no planning is complete without "bag" assembly time.

My Own Bag (Ages Two and Up)

The bag can be bought or made. It can be an old purse or a plastic sack. One mother's "bag" idea was a metal cake pan with a sliding cover. She said it was an excelled container for pencils, paper, crayons, scissors, books, and activity books. And the top doubled as a writing surface!

Another clever mother used paper bags and let her kids decorate two bags each.

The important thing is that each child have his/her own bag (cake pan or whatever!) with appropriate items for his/her age level. Some bag filler ideas are:

- paper tablet
- colored pencils
- colored markers
- coloring book
- dot-to-dot book
- activity book
- sticker book
- sewing cards

- magic slate
- small cars
- Scotch tape
- pretty stickers
- Band-Aids (You'd be amazed at what one child can do with one box of Band-Aids!)
- books
- favorite stuffed animal or doll
- scissors
- flashlight and extra batteries (this can be a fun toy as well as a bedtime security in a strange room)
- card games
- glue stick (Be sure to get a stick and not "gooey" glue!)

Usually our children's bags were filled with items they already enjoyed. Sometimes we bought one or two new treasures for their bags, but most new travel treasures came from Mom's Surprise Bag.

Mom's Surprise Bag

"A surprise a day keeps tears and quarrels away!" (at least some of the time). It also adds an air of expectation to each travel day. Designate a special time each day—two or three in the afternoon is usually a time when travelers begin to feel grumpy and weary of sitting—for the ceremony of the day's treasure.

What treasures does Mom store in her surprise bag? They can be big or small, expensive or cheap, wrapped or unwrapped, something to play with, to make, or to eat. The selection is limited only by your

119

creativity and budget! An important ingredient is that the surprise is right for the age and ability level of your child.

Some surprises we used include:

- hook rug kit
- sugarless gum (a whole pack for each child)
- flashlight and batteries
- books
- comic books
- leather-making kit
- tapes with music
- magic erasable slate
- sewing cards
- colored pencils and paper
- a new pencil and eraser
- cute pad of paper
- activity books
- punch-out paper dolls
- Scotch tape
- small toy
- bag of balloons
- deck of cards
- doodle art
- magnetic chess set
- needlepoint or cross-stitch kit
- Mini-Mastermind game
- magnetic checker set
- Trouble Bubble game
- travel bingo

Anything listed under "my own bag" is perfect for Mom's Surprise Bag too. Although children love to get sweets, we've found activity-oriented gifts the best, as they give them something to do. We collect "bargain surprises" throughout the year for Mom's Surprise Travel Bag, so they are always on hand for impromptu trips.

One mom added this tip—for games, check out the birthday party favors at your favorite toy store. Kids love that junk and it's fairly inexpensive.

A note of warning! When choosing surprises, remember that marbles roll, crayons and chocolate melt, chalk crumbles, bubble gum gets stuck in hair, and small toy parts get lost!

Mom's Own Bag

We've planned for the children—their own "bag" and Mom's Surprise Bag full of goodies that will warm their hearts and possibly help them sit still. Now, Mom needs a bag for Mom! Begin with a "surprise" for you—a new book or whatever you'd like. Then add the essentials for triumphant travel.

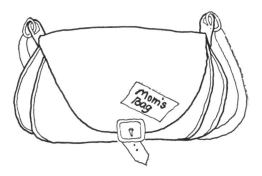

- paper towels
- pre-moistened towels
- lots of Band-Aids
- jump rope for everyone to exercise while stopping for gas, etc.
- timer for changing seat assignments
- water jug and paper cups
- large and small plastic bags (for garbage, motion sickness, dirty laundry, wet bathing suits, etc.)

Food Bag—A Must!

Whether traveling by plane, bus, car, or train, eating will be a major activity on any trip. Regardless of the games or activities you plan, food will be a star attraction. *Be prepared*—food requests often come fifteen minutes after you leave home! Chips, candy, cookies, and all "the junkies" will of course be well received, but first think about protein snacks and fruits such as:

- hard-cooked eggs
- cheeses
- raisins
- nuts (a mix of peanuts, almonds, and raisins is a favorite of our families)
- peanut butter, to spread on crackers, bread, bananas, or celery

- carrot and celery sticks (immersed in cold water for a long trip, otherwise just washed and packed in a plastic bag)
- apples, oranges, tangerines, and bananas
- granola bars
- gorp (a mixture of peanuts, raisins, and M&M's)
- mixture of sunflower seeds, peanuts, and raisins
- sunflower seeds

To avoid messes and disagreements, try putting combo mixes like the raisin-peanut-hazelnut-almond mixture in individual plastic bags. Popcorn is also a favorite, packed for each child in individual bags.

The Food Bag must also have drinks! One wise mother (not popular, but wise!) carried only ice-cold water while traveling. Spilled, it wasn't sticky and it didn't stain. Since water is less appealing than sweetened drinks, it was requested less often and subsequent "potty stops" were fewer. Here are some more exciting drink suggestions.

1. Small individual cans of juice. These can be frozen beforehand and allowed to thaw along the way. They are delicious and ice cold.

2. Tupperware plastic glasses with spill-proof lids are great for drinks en route. They can be filled with juice or just ice cubes that will melt along the way and provide ice water.

3. Try thermos or camper canteens for a personal drinking container for each child. Then *they* decide when to have a drink and are not constantly saying, "Mommy, I'm thirsty!"

The Music Machine

Another planning tip is to consider incorporating music into your summer trips. Favorite songs sung together make distances seem shorter and give enjoyment to all. Why not take a couple of songbooks on your next trip and learn new songs as you travel?

Our families always traveled with a cassette tape recorder and tapes. Today most cars come equipped with a tape deck. When our children were younger, we carried tapes of children's songs and found they were perfect for those times when everyone was all "gamed out" or "sung out" and there were still many miles to go. Christian albums like the Bill Gaither *I'm a Promise* and *Especially for Children* are great to soothe nerves. *The Music Machine* doesn't soothe nerves but it is a super children's tape for teaching the fruit of the Spirit—love, joy, peace, patience—that are all especially needed in the car!

Our friends with young children recommend:

- Glad Tapes
- Integrity Tapes
- Psaltry Tapes
- *Patch the Pirate* (*Patch* tapes can be ordered from Musical Ministries, Inc., P.O. Box 6524, Greenville, SC 29606.)

One young mother suggested starting an informal "lending library" among friends. "It's easy to spend $10.00 for just one tape," Cary said. "Before we take a trip, I visit my friends and borrow books and tapes that my children haven't heard. I offer to loan our tapes and books to other families. I'm helping others while modeling to my own children the importance of sharing. It also really helps our limited budget."

We liked to carry along a blank tape for taping our own singing or recording our own stories. Before trips we often taped our favorite records and stories. The children especially enjoyed tapes of *Black Beauty* and *Treasure Island*. (Even the adults enjoy hearing the stories again and again, and especially the silence and absence of bickering when all ears are listening!)

PLANNING ACCOMPLISHED!

Travel time will be wonderfully different (even fun!) when you plan ahead. Taking the time to assemble all the "bags" (Children's Own Bag, Mom's Surprise Bag, Mom's Own Bag, and Food Bag) will make you as prepared as a good Girl Scout. Helping your children make a Travel Notebook will improve their spelling, writing, research, and organizational abilities, and it probably will add an air of excitement about the trip.

We all have our "bags" and our children have their notebooks, but now the trip has begun and we all must sit for eight to ten hours a day. *Help!*

Structure Your Day

Particularly helpful with younger children, but also good for older ones, is to add structure to your long days of travel. A typical structured day might be:

9 A.M.   Read a Bible story or Christian book to children.

10 A.M. One parent gets in back seat (if possible) and plays a game with the children.

11 A.M. Cassette time—If children are old enough, let them use recorder by themselves.

12 P.M. Lunch.

1 P.M.   Children play games alone or with parents. (The list that follows will give you lots of ideas.)

2 P.M.   Mom's Surprise Bag time! Then children play with surprises.

3 P.M.   Parent or older child reads aloud from a book. Plan to read several chapters from the book every day at this time.

4 P.M.   Snack time!

5 P.M.   If you still have miles to go, turn on the "soothing music" and pray!

Of course, the day can have as little or as much structure as you feel your children need. Variety and structure help keep the children's minds and hands occupied so you hear less frequently, "When will we be there?"

If you run out of games to play, try some of these.

Games People Play

1. *Name That Tune* (ages three and up). One person hums the melody or claps out the rhythm of a song, and the other players must guess the song. Even very small children can play this game if simple songs for children are chosen.

2. *Collecting Your Years* (ages four and up). The players decide on an object—a church, a train, a certain kind of car. Each player has to find as many as he is years old—four for a four-year-old, eight for an eight-year-old. Everyone who finds his number is a winner!

3. *Silly Stories.* Each player tells one line or one paragraph of a story. You make it up as you go along and continue it as long as you like.

4. *Poor Puppy* (ages three and up, but best for younger children). One player, the "puppy," makes faces or funny noises. One at a time, the other players pat the puppy on the head and say, "Poor puppy" three

times without laughing. If the "patter" laughs, he/she becomes the puppy.

5. *Four Is the Score* (ages six and up). One player says to another player, "Name four rivers." If he can't, the first player has another turn. He then asks him to name four of something else (cars, states, cities, trees, names that begin with K). When he can name four, it's his turn to ask for four. Each player who asks for four things must be able to name them himself. If he asks for four of something that he can't answer, he loses his next turn.

6. *Elf Hide-and-Seek* (ages three and up). The first player says, "I'm an elf, only three inches tall. Where am I hiding?" The other players have to guess where someone three inches tall could be hiding. "In the Food Bag?" "No." "In the Surprise Bag?" "No." "In Daddy's pocket?" "Yes!" The next elf can be two inches tall, or any size he chooses.

7. *Macaroni* (ages four and up). Think of something you like to do, like swimming. The other players have to guess it. They ask you questions, and because they don't know your word they have to use the word "macaroni" instead. For example: "Does everybody macaroni?" No. "Have you ever macaronied?" Yes. "Do you macaroni outside?" Yes. The questions go on until somebody guesses that "macaroni" is swimming.

8. *Quaker Meeting* (three years and up). Nobody talks, giggles, or makes a sound. First to do so loses. (This is a short but effective activity when the noise level has become unbearable!)

9. *Road Map Charting* (ages eight and older). Give each child a road map of the route you are traveling. As you travel, have them mark your route with highlight markers to help the driver check his progress.

10. *Appoint Record-Keeper* (ages eight and older). Children can become involved in helping keep records, and they also can learn a great deal about math without realizing it. They can record:

- Number of miles traveled in an hour, a day, or the whole trip;
- Amount of gasoline used, cost, and miles per gallon (Have handkerchief handy, should Dad begin to weep uncontrollably!);
- Meals eaten and their cost.

11. *Acronyms* (ages eight and up). The letters on license plates sometimes spell words, or they can be arranged to spell words. Or they can be acronyms:

HTC = High Tension Cable

GOG = Good Old Goat
WSM = WOW! SUPER MOM!

12. *New Name Game* (ages three and up). The players all decide on a new name. For the next sixty miles each player *must* be called by his new name. If a player forgets and uses a real name, a point is scored against him. The winner is the player with the lowest score at the end of the sixty miles.

13. *Alphabet Trip* (ages five and up). One player begins the game by saying something like, "My name is *Allison*, I'm taking a trip to *Africa*, and I'm going to bring back some *animals*." (All the words start with *A*.) The next player uses the letter *B* and says something like, "My name is Bob, I'm going to Bangladesh, and I'm going to bring back some bottles." All the players take turns, using different letters of the alphabet. (Leave out the letter *X*, as it is difficult.)

14. *Stinky Pinky* (ages eight and up). This is a fun rhyming word game that will help the miles go by quickly! It is a great game for older children and adults. The little tots enjoy listening and taking "their turn" too—although with them the rules must be modified (or ignored).

One person thinks of two words that rhyme, like "green bean." Then two clues are given. The first clue is the number of syllables in each word—this is where the name of the game comes in. If the mystery words have two syllables each, then it is a "stinky pinky." If the mystery words only have one syllable each, it is a "stink pink." Three syllables each makes it a "stinkety pinkety."

If one person has chosen "green bean," he would first give this clue: "I'm thinking of a stink pink."

The second clue is two words that describe the hidden words. For "green bean" the clue could be "colored vegetable," so the person would say, "I'm thinking of a stink pink and it is a colored vegetable." Then the others must guess until someone comes up with the correct rhyming words, "green bean." Let the person who guesses it right have the next turn, or take turns in a specified manner.

Think up your own combinations or use the ones below to get you started. Before the trip you could write them out on paper, fold them, and put them in an envelope for just the right moment when the children say, "We're bored; what can we do?"

Stink Pinks	*Clue*
roast toast	cooked bread
dumb gum	unintelligent chew

fox box	animal container
hi bye	hello, so long
silk milk	fabric drink
hot pot	heated utensil
heard bird	singing robin
top pop	great dad

Stinky Pinky	*Clue*
able table	capable furniture
hour flower	timed plant
better sweater	improved wrap

| *Stinkety Pinkety* | *Clue* |
| concentration education | focused learning |

| *Stinkety Pinky* | *Clue* |
| malfunction junction | mixed-up intersection |

Roget's New Pocket Thesaurus can be a valuable aid in this game. Why not stick it in "Mom's Bag"?

TRIUMPHANT TRAVELING

As you, along with families all over America, hit the vacation trails this summer, committed to having family fun (no matter how much pain and suffering it entails), your hours in the car, train, or planes can be triumphant! Remember to be prepared, which means to *plan*.

Researching and making Travel Notebooks builds enthusiasm. Mom's Bags keep boredom and hunger away. Children's Bags add variety; music soothes; structure adds sanity; and games are just plain fun! With these tips applied, you just might agree that traveling with children can be fun!

CHAPTER 12

A Special Word to Wives...
Husbands Have
Summers Too

We've spent quite a few pages talking about fitting our children into our summers. What about our husbands? Too often when we think of including them in our summers, we think of baby-sitting. One husband reluctantly volunteered to watch his four small children on a Saturday. Being a statistician, he took copious notes, and when his wife returned he gave her a list that read:

Dried tears—11 times
Tied shoelaces—15 times
Blew up toy balloons—5 per child
Average life of each balloon—10 seconds
Warned children not to run across street—26 times
Number of Saturdays I will go through this again—0!

Husbands need to fit into our summers too. Perhaps sometimes it *will* be as a baby-sitter, but there are many more exciting ways! Too often, marriages reflect the attitude of the woman who said, "Marriage begins when you sink into his arms and ends with your arms in the sink." This summer let's get our arms out of our sinks and around our mates!

"YOU'RE SOMETHING SPECIAL!"

How can we show our husbands this summer that they are special? In our list of priorities we would never say with words that our children are more important to us than our husbands, but in our actions this can easily be true. Many times our children's needs come first. There *are* times when we must tend to the urgent. Spilled orange juice left unattended can become a sticky mess, and crying, hungry children cannot be ignored. But beyond the surface of the immediate needs there should be a basic attitude—"Honey, you are the most important person in my life. I may be cleaning up orange juice, but you still are first!"

An eleven-year-old boy put it this way:

> My mother keeps a cookie jar in the kitchen and we can help ourselves, except we can't if it is too close to meal times. Only my dad can any time. When he comes home from the office, he helps himself no matter if it is just before we eat. He always brags about how great she is and how good she can cook. Then she turns around and they hug. The way they do it you would think they just got married or something. It makes me feel good. This is what I like best about our home.[1]

Our First Love

Psychologists say the most important thing a mother can do for her child is to love the child's father, and the most important thing a father can do for his child is to love the child's mother. A child can be loved by both the mother and the father, but if Mommy and Daddy don't love each other a child can have deep feelings of insecurity. One son said it this way to his father:

> When I was younger, I didn't realize why your taking Mom out to eat alone made me feel so good. But it was like one of the many reassuring signs of the love between you. I can remember the jolt I felt the first time I heard you say that you loved each other more than any of us kids. I can also remember thinking that out and realizing how fortunate it is. After all, we are products of that love. So seeing it expressed was bound to make us all the more secure.[2]

What can you do to show your husband (and children) this summer that he is Number One? If you don't plan your husbands into your summer, your schedules will easily become "too busy," and all he will get is the tired leftovers. And we've found that after a full summer day with three active children, there is little left over! Remember: One of your goals is to get to know your husband more intimately this summer.

Build Your Team

How can you begin? By letting your mate know you're on his team! Whether his "thing" is golf, tennis, jogging, bowling, or chess; get off the sidelines! A friend's husband is an avid fisherman. When they were first married, he suggested they go fishing. Because she had heard that the family that plays together stays together, she went. The first time she put a minnow on a fishing hook, she was sure she would vomit. As with most things, however, it got easier, and soon she could do it without closing her eyes!

Now, many years and four children later, she is thankful she became involved in her husband's interests. Recently she confided, "Do you know the best time Bruce and I had last year? It was at six in the morning, cleaning fish by the lake. The children were asleep, and we talked of deep and wonderful things we rarely talk about. I thanked God that morning that I had been willing to put that first minnow on the hook."

What's your minnow? Let's look carefully this summer at the special man God has given you to love. Find one common interest that needs developing. It's great to be a "cheerleader," but it's better yet to be on his team!

SUMMER SPECIALS FOR YOUR MAN

Summer Dating

One thing we still plan into our summer is dating. We choose one night a week as our standing date night. There are times when it doesn't work out as scheduled, but we do it more often than if we didn't plan it into our summer weeks. Perhaps for some it's more realistic to set a goal of two dates per summer month. This would provide six wonderful times to look forward to! Actually, this is something we try to do year round with our husbands, and it has really been a help in keeping communications open.

We have two goals for our times alone: (1) communication, and staying on the same wavelength, and (2) having fun together! We try to vary what we do on dates, and we've found that there are lots of different possibilities, many of them inexpensive. Why not collect "date ideas"? We've talked to too many women who say they are tired of always going out to dinner and a movie. We think part of the solution lies in knowing each other's interests and in being willing to try new things.

A friend and her husband love antiques and decided to visit auctions together on dates. Here are some of the things we have tried.

- Go out for ice cream and a long conversation.
- Go for a hike in the woods.
- Play a game of tennis.
- Go on a picnic.
- Visit a museum and then stop off for coffee and talking.

- Borrow someone's vacant apartment or house and have a private dinner for two.
- When the children were younger and we had no baby-sitter, we would put them to bed early and then have a "candlelight dinner date."
- Go bike riding.
- Go for a drive in the country.
- Read a book together and discuss it.

For a series of dates that will build your marriage, see Dave and Claudia Arp's book, *Ten Dates for Mates*.

If we are really committed to spending time alone together with our husbands, then with a lot of creativity and perseverance it will happen. It's definitely not something that comes easily, but it adds a new dimension to marriage (and summer sanity) that is well worth all the effort it takes!

Vacation for Two

Linda recalls one rainy Friday. "My plan was to take Jody away to a lake cabin for the weekend. He was speaking at a marriage conference, and I was to join him and speak to the women that evening. All during the day, I set my plan in motion and prepared to go. I packed suitcases, bought food, and cleaned the house. Everything went wrong—I didn't feel good, everything took longer than I had planned, and the children whined and said they didn't want me to go. I felt miserable. As I drove across town in the rain, I cried and thought, *It's not worth all the effort. Why am I doing this anyway?*

"After arriving at the conference, I spoke for three hours and was very tired. Why had I planned for us to go away? Jody and I walked to the car that night and, opening the door, he saw the suitcases.

"'What are these for?' he asked.

"'Honey, I'm whisking you away to a lake cabin for the weekend,' I answered.

"All I needed was the look on his face! Do you know that I forgot all the tears and the hassle to get ready? Our two days were wonderful—just what we both needed. It was worth the effort!"

Claudia remembers a great summer experience. "Good friends called and offered us their mountain home while they were away on a trip. The boys were at Boy Scout camp for the week, so we packed our bags and headed for the mountains. What a fantastic week that was . . . sleeping late in the mornings, breakfast at eleven, hiking through the mountains in the afternoons with no time deadlines, hours and hours to talk and love and play!

"It's not always possible to take a whole week away, but even to get away for twenty-four hours works wonders."

You may be thinking, *That's great for you, but you don't know my situation—my husband, our finances, etc. There is just no way!* We agree that it's not *easy,* and many times our good plans fall through—a child gets sick or a husband's schedule is changed. But please believe us when we say it's worth it.

Tips for Taking Time Away

To help make a vacation for two a reality, consider some things we have tried successfully.

- Swapping children with a good friend for a weekend away. There are no baby-sitting fees to pay, and the children enjoy being with their friends. (Yes, it's work for the baby-sitting mother, but it's worth it because she gets a turn too!)
- Take advantage of the week the children are at summer camp, visiting grandparents, etc.
- Borrow an empty house or cabin while friends are away.
- Prepare food to take along for some of the meals to cut down on cost.
- Take off your watch when you get there and concentrate on enjoying one another.
- Go alone!
- Leave work at home. We encouraged one friend to plan a vacation for two with her husband. When we saw Mary several months later she was very excited. They had stolen away to a friend's empty house for two days and nights and had gotten caught up on all their correspondence! (This was not exactly what we had in mind.)
- We both love to go away with our husbands and just relax and live an unstructured life for a couple of days. But if you prefer more structure, plan some communication games and exercises to stimulate communication. One we recommend is the Ungame. We have found the Ungame a useful tool to get couples talking and listening to one another and to enhance listening and communication skills in marriage.
- Choose a book on marriage and read it before your time alone. Then discuss it together. Some we recommend are:

1. *Ten Dates for Mates* by Dave and Claudia Arp (Thomas Nelson).
2. *Secret Choices* and *Intended for Pleasure* by Ed Wheat (Revell).
3. *60 One-Minute Marriage Builders* by Dave and Claudia Arp (Wolgemuth & Hyatt).
4. *Solomon on Sex* by Joseph Dillow (Thomas Nelson).
5. *The Marriage Builder* by Larry Crabb (BMH).

A Summer Love Affair

What creative ways can we express our love and make our marriages more exciting love affairs this summer? Maybe with a special gift given for no reason at all.

"I will always remember one February third," says Linda. "It stands out in my mind as a special day! It wasn't my birthday or our anniversary, we hadn't had a quarrel, and Valentine's Day was eleven days away. There was no reason for my husband to give me a gift.

"I walked into our house cold and tired that February third, and there on the table was an envelope of money, along with a note that said, 'Honey, I've been saving so you could have that clock you've wanted. I love you. Jody.' No reason for the gift, except 'I love you!' I can't tell you how much that little envelope full of dollars, quarters, and dimes meant to me. It meant so much because there was no reason to give it, no special day needing to be observed, no advertisers prompting husbands to remember."

Perhaps the best gifts of all are those freely given. Maybe we should plan a surprise gift for June 10 or July 6 or August 23, just to say "I love you!"

And gifts don't have to be expensive! One man, plagued with financial difficulties, had nothing to give his wife on their anniversary. But on their anniversary morning this clever man woke his wife with a beautiful breakfast tray, a single long-stemmed rose, and a hand-drawn card with this inscription:

"Happy anniversary, darling! In lieu of a gift, contributions have been made in your name to the electric company, the phone company, and three department stores!"

A special summer "I love you" could be so many things—a gift, a favorite pie, dinner for two, a homemade card, and on and on.

133

Cards for Reading

One friend, whose husband went on to graduate school after several years of working, tried to let him know the family was behind him and that they knew he could make the grade. Each Thursday she made a clever card and put it in his lunch on Friday. The theme of the card was usually, "Hooray, it's the weekend. You're home with us!" She did this for months, and her husband *never* commented on her creative cards. Then one Thursday she was very busy and didn't make the card. At noon on Friday the phone rang. "Where's my card?" her husband wanted to know.

We need to remember that the motivation in whatever we do for our husbands should not be to get a response from them. Rather, it should be because we want to be faithful to God and love our husbands unconditionally. It's easy to want that response from our husbands and to give up quickly when the response doesn't come.

Coupons for Cashing

Remember the coupon book suggestion for time alone with your children? How about adapting the idea for use with your husband? Be as creative as you want to be. To start you thinking, here are some coupon ideas we have used with our husbands (at least, some that aren't too personal to print!).

- Good for candlelight dinner for two
  (present coupon twenty-four hours in advance)

- Good for one morning of sleeping in, with breakfast in bed
- Good for one back rub with heated oil
- Good for going out for coffee and dessert whenever you want
- Good for a steak dinner for two at your favorite restaurant (I pay!)
- Good for lunch together—you choose the place (you pay!)

LET'S BEGIN

We've shared four ways to include our husbands in our summers:

1. Summer dates
2. Vacations for two
3. Special summertime "I love you" surprises
4. Coupons for cashing

Now that we have lots of ideas for our children and our husbands, what about us? In the next chapter we will see that moms have summers too!

CHAPTER 13

Summer Strategies
for Mom

"Summertime and the living is easy" are lyrics with which few mothers can identify. Besides your plans for Children's Day, "Just-Me-and-Mom" time, and summer dates with Dad, you already have a schedule as full as any corporate executive's. After all, you are responsible for food services, purchasing, building and grounds, motor pool, personnel, and public relations (including birthday parties, outdoor cookouts, and formal entertaining).

Your working hours are unbelievable. You need no alarm clock as your young children faithfully begin their summer days at six-thirty—very, very loudly! Your older children don't begin their day quite as early (actually, much later), but they require your availability later in the evening (checking to see that they are home and their responsibilities are all carried out). And if you are a working or a single parent, you can probably double your stress level.

Unless you are a whiz of an organizer and possess the energy and drive of a bulldozer, it's likely that whatever your own situation, you will regularly fall behind and continually be overwhelmed. You may be thinking, *Find time for myself? Are you crazy? Grow as a person this summer? Develop a new interest? Why, I'll be happy just to survive!*

SANITY OR SURVIVAL?

This is a book about summertime sanity, not just survival. So what can we do? It would be wonderful if we had each day to schedule just as we wished, and our family and friends would adjust their plans to fit ours. But alas, it is not to be!

Reluctantly, we have to admit that inevitably some time must be spent on activities outside our control. We don't have twenty-four hours a day to live as we choose. Interruptions are a summer household word.

There is *no way* we can do everything. So what do we do? Too often when we plan our schedules, we go to one extreme or the other, like the weekly plans of Mom A and Mom B.

Mom A's schedule for the summer looks like this:
Monday—Go swimming with children, take them to ballet lessons, have three friends of children spend the night.
Tuesday—All-day picnic with the children and their friends at the lake.
Wednesday—Children's Day—Neighborhood circus in backyard. I make the refreshments. Children's tennis lessons in afternoon.
Thursday—Take children out to brunch and a movie.
Friday—Children's soccer games all morning. Then afternoon at the zoo.
Saturday—Trip to the country with the children.
Sunday—Sunday school, church, then collapse.

Mom B's schedule is very different.
Monday—I play tennis; take children to YMCA program.
Tuesday—Creative writing course, then bridge. Get baby-sitter.
Wednesday—Community concerns women's meeting. Lunch with Fran. Get baby-sitter.
Thursday—Bible study, lunch with Cindy. Get baby-sitter.
Friday—Drop kids at summer program. Spend day with Marg and Fran planning tennis tournament.
Saturday—Morning at church—organizing banquet for tonight.
Sunday—Sunday school, church, afternoon tennis. Husband can baby-sit.

It's easy to see the opposite extremes in these two mothers' schedules. Mom A is totally child-oriented, while Mom B's summer plans are self-oriented. Mom A has forgotten that parents have summers too, and Mom B has forgotten her children!

BE A PRIORITY PLANNER

We believe the key to keeping the right balance in our lives this summer is to choose the right priorities and schedule our time to reflect those priorities. We've given lots of suggestions in this book for making summer sane, but if your priorities are out of order, all your good planning will be to no avail!

Here is a list of our priorities, but for a more detailed look please refer to *Creative Counterpart* by Linda Dillow, Chapter 4.

1. God
2. Husband
3. Children
4. Home
5. Yourself
6. Outside your home

If you are a single parent, adapt your priority list for your very own situation—of course, God and your children will take the top places. You have to decide how to juggle home and work and other activities. We hope the practical helps in this book will encourage you and help you find a good balance.

We've seen how our relationship with our family can grow this summer by spending quality time with them. In the same way, our relationship with God will grow as we put Him first in our lives and spend time with Him.

In this chapter we want to look at how we can keep God first in our lives this summer. Then we will look at how to find time for ourselves— how we can be stretched as persons.

Who Runs the "Holy Hurdles"?

One of the biggest and most common mistakes women make is to substitute *activity* for God for a *relationship* with Him. On the outside we're busy running the "holy hurdles," but on the inside our relationship with Christ is at a standstill.

When Jesus comes to visit Mary and Martha and Lazarus, we find Mary sitting at His feet to learn from Him (see Luke 10:39). Mary is mentioned five times in the New Testament, and each time we find her at the feet of Jesus.

And then we see Martha. She's scurrying around, as many of us would be—preparing food, attending to the guests, tidying the house, organizing things. Martha's contributions were important, yet when she complained to Jesus that Mary was not helping her, He replied that Mary had chosen what is better.

Christ was not saying that organizing, cooking, and serving are not important. They are, and we can receive much joy from doing these things. Yet all the activity in the world will never give us the peace and joy of a vital relationship with Jesus Christ. We need to spend time sitting at Jesus' feet this summer.

Into the Closet

The best time to build your relationship with Christ through prayer and Bible study is during a devotional time. How we struggle with this! We manage to carve out the time for maybe a week, and then we give up. Perhaps one reason for our failure is that we set our goals too high: "I'll be up every morning at five!" By the third day we're so exhausted that we can't even *find* the Bible, let alone *study* it!

God wants us to be realistic. Evaluate your life and set a goal that is possible for you to achieve. Don't feel guilty if you read about some dear saint who gets up at five every morning to pray for her nine children! A devotional time is not a law, but a relationship, and your relationship with the Savior will be different from everyone else's.

Your Quiet Time is a time for you to draw apart with God. It is a special time for you to talk with Him about the events of the day, your growth in Him, your concerns, your blessings. A Quiet Time is not a time to quietly prepare your Sunday school lesson. Neither is it a time to browse through a church magazine or even to write to a missionary.

It is a time set aside to deepen your knowledge of the Lord, to enrich your own personal relationship with Him, to fellowship with Him, to love Him, to worship Him on a very personal basis. This time each day is for *your own personal growth* in the Lord. No matter how old you are in the Lord or how closely you walk with Him, this time of intimacy will always be necessary.

PRACTICALLY SPEAKING

In choosing your summer strategy for spiritual growth, try the following.

1. Pick a time. We suggest taking at least fifteen minutes a day to spend alone with God. It's great if you can find half an hour, or maybe even an hour. The amount of time may vary from day to day, but the important thing is to spend time with Him on a regular basis.

2. Pick a place—living room, bedroom, or favorite chair.

3. Pick an emphasis. One summer we decided to emphasize good interpersonal communication, and the long, hot, humid days of family togetherness gave us many opportunities for instant application!

If this area is a need in your life (and if you're a parent, we assume it is!), then we have two practical suggestions for you this summer. Following are two projects we have done to keep our relationship with the Lord a vital and growing one and to help us in relating to our families.

Take Your Temperature

We began by comparing our words and responses with God's standard. Let's look at Colossians 3:12–15 and see what God has to say about communication. These verses seem to deal with our attitude and how we're coming across.

> And so, as those who have been chosen of God, holy and beloved, put on a heart of compassion, kindness, humility, gentleness and patience; bearing with one another, and forgiving each other, whoever has a complaint against any one; just as the Lord forgave you, so also should you. And beyond all these things put on love, which is the perfect bond of unity. And let the peace of Christ rule in your hearts, to which indeed you were called in one body; and be thankful.

To make these verses real and practical, we put them in chart form. First, we listed the different characteristics of good communication from Colossians 3. Then we listed our husbands' and children's names.

We used the chart for several days, and at the end of each day we scored ourselves to see how we were doing. We found there was plenty of room for improvement!

At the end of the day, score yourself on a scale of 1 to 5:

1—Bravo! Keep talking, Mom!

2—Definitely on the right track!

3—Okay, but don't put away the mouth muzzle yet!

4—Improvement needed! Reread Colossians 3!

5—Improvement desperately needed! Put on mouth muzzle and memorize Colossians 3!

Taking our temperature in this way made us more aware of how we were coming across and helped us to "keep our cool" and actually show compassion, kindness, patience, forgiveness, and love when we were tempted to blow it. Like the time Joel came home too late for dinner and missed an important Boy Scout meeting. Or when Tommy missed soccer practice because his soccer shoes were left at the store that morning. Or when Jonathan left his ski boots on the bus. Or when our husbands were late and forgot to call and let us know. Becoming aware of how

	Dave	Jarrett	Joel	Jonathan
Compassion				
Kindness				
Humility				
Gentleness				
Patience				
Forgiveness				
Love				

we're coming across and evaluating our communication by God's thermometer is a first step to improving in this area this summer.

Take your temperature once a week this summer, and memorize Colossians 3:12–15. God's Word is living and will live in us this summer as we study His Word and make Him our number-one priority.

Do a Topical Study from Proverbs on Communication

To help you learn more about what God's Word says about communication, a topical study from Proverbs and other helps for a summer Quiet Time are given in Appendix II.

MOM'S DAY FOR MOM

We've planned a Children's Day into each summer week, a day of fun togetherness getting to know our five-ring circuses better. Now let's plan a special day for Mom so that we can get to know her better and find out more about *her* interests, desires, and areas of expertise. We know that we're better mothers if we have goals for ourselves and some time away from the children. Much is said today about mothers not having a "self-identity." Perhaps part of the reason is that we try to be like Mom A and keep no time or set no goals for ourselves.

A Mom's Day is *not* a time to grocery shop, go to the cleaners, or clean out a closet. It *is* time away from children, home, and responsibilities to work toward a personal goal for ourselves. It can be a morning, an afternoon, or better yet an entire day. The only necessity is that you do it.

How do you have a Mom's Day?

1. You pray
2. You plan
   a. For a baby-sitter to come regularly.
   b. To trade children with a friend. Perhaps you have her tribe on Tuesday while she has her Mom's Day, and she has yours on Thursday.

We have tried regular baby-sitters and trading children, and both have worked well.

What do you do on Mom's Day? Here are some examples.

Linda: "One summer I set a goal to learn to macramé, and I made several plant hangers for Christmas gifts. There is a certain exhilaration that comes when your Christmas gifts are ready before September! Another summer my goal was to finish writing *Creative Counterpart,* and two mornings a week I stole away to a friend's vacant apartment to write."

Claudia: "Having a vegetable garden was a project I picked one summer. It was so much fun to pick a head of lettuce and make a fresh green salad, all within minutes. The boys even ate turnip greens because we grew them! (They put them between two pieces of bread with catsup and made a turnip green sandwich! Ugh!) One summer I concentrated on making two new outfits for fall. I love to sew but have trouble finding the time. Having a Mom's Day sewing time provided the time."

The key for us has been choosing *one* project for the summer and sticking to it. Majoring on one goal gives us more assurance of accomplishing it. Skipping from project to project throughout the summer assures only frustration and unattained goals.

BE A LIST-MAKER

Before those hot summer days arrive, make a list of *all* the things you would like to do. Get all your ideas down on paper and then carefully choose one project as your goal. You can't write a book, take a course, play in a tennis league, make all your Christmas presents, and learn gourmet cooking in one summer!

One woman divided her list of possible goals into the categories of physical, intellectual, and new-skill goals.

I. Physical Goals
  A. Start an exercise program
  B. Learn a new sport (tennis, swimming, golf, jogging)
  C. Improve personal appearance
    1. Lose ten pounds
    2. Change makeup, hairstyle, etc.
    3. Work on wardrobe
II. Intellectual Goals
  A. Take an art history course
  B. Take a Bible correspondence course
  C. Study a foreign language
  D. Join a book club or start a personal reading program
  E. Study current events
  F. Take a creative writing course
  G. Take a computer course
III. New-Skill Goals
  A. Learn to macramé, crochet, knit, or needlepoint
  B. Take piano lessons
  C. Learn to sew
  D. Have a vegetable garden
  E. Learn to wallpaper

After listing all her areas of interest under these three headings, she realized it would take years to do them all! So since she felt she needed most to be stretched intellectually, she decided to take an art history course at the local university. Her Thursday Mom's Day would involve:

9:00—12:00—attend class at the university
12:00—2:00—meet friend for lunch
2:00—4:00—study material for course at the library

Perhaps in the fall she would pick another goal, this time from the physical or new-skill areas.

The ultimate summer planning for Mom would involve choosing a goal from all three areas: intellectual, physical, and new-skill. If this is possible, great, but be sure to plan realistically for your Mom's Day so that at summer's end you can look with satisfaction at a project or projects completed.

Now, make your own list and choose a summer project "just for Mom." Then get ready to put it all together, and plan out your summer strategy!

IT'S YOUR TIME, MOM!

Now is the time to remember that forgotten dream or secret desire, to get the tennis racket out of the attic or the art kit out of moth balls, or to dust off that university catalog on the top shelf of the bookcase. Perhaps now is the time to see a hidden desire become a reality. When we begin to work on a goal—even for just a small amount of time each week—we take it out of the realm of fantasy and make it reality.

One husband put it this way, "I find my wife much more attractive and stimulating when she has interests outside the home—when she is growing and being stretched as a person."

Not only will our mates and friends find us more interesting as we choose a challenge or growth area this summer, but come September we'll be able to look back on our summer and say, "I am growing. I am learning. I am accomplishing something. I am developing as a person!"

CHAPTER 14

Walking the Two-Job Tightrope— Extra Helps for Working and/or Single Parents[1]

Ode to Working Mothers

When Michelangelo hung from ceilings
When Polo was studying his maps
Did they have to call it a day
When the children got up from their naps?

Could David have perfected his slingshot
Or Moses taken off for the hills
If they'd been president of the PTA
Or had 2-year-olds with fever and chills?

While Einstein was figuring equations,
While Beethoven was humming a sonata,
Did the day-care people ever call up
To say, "It's 5! Your baby! You forgot her?"

If Plato had been the family nurse,
Scrubber of sinks and such,
How much time would he have had
To think? To write? Not much.

While Michael Jordan was slam-dunking,
While Babe Ruth was rounding the bases,
Did they have to stop in their tracks
To wipe tears off little sad faces?

Would his thinking be so positive
If the Rev. Norman Vincent Peale
Had to find something everyone could eat
Every single meal?

If Shakespeare had had teenagers to mind
His brain would have been too tired for sonnets
And Bell couldn't have invented the telephone
'Cause his daughter would always be on it.

All history would be rewritten, I guess,
With lots of new stories to tell
If our forefathers had not only their work to do—
But a mother's job as well.

> Ina Hughs
> *News-Sentinel* staff writer[2]

It was a simple statement with only a hint of malice.

"When school's out, Nathan gets to stay home and play with his toys all day," my friend's son said, as he briefly glanced up to check for Mom's response.

Sarcastically his mother thought, but didn't say, "You poor little dear, you have to spend all summer at day care going to movies, skating, swimming, and taking field trips to theme parks. I know the schedule; I wrote the check." But no comment at all seemed the best response.

Being a single parent isn't easy, especially when we think of the summertime. My friend has covered the "why Mommy works" scenario before. She and her son had talked about it at the beginning of the school year when they discussed why he had to ride the van to day care and couldn't be a "car rider." She had also explained that mother just doesn't do the guilt routine, so he could just skip the woeful expressions.

Even with that proclamation, in her heart she knew that the beginning of summer stirs up the little black guilt clouds in dual-career and single-parent families.

While there are added pressures and time crunches for working and single parents, some solutions can actually relieve that heavy dose of guilt if they are approached with a desire to make summer special for everyone.

While we contend that all parents are "working parents," some have the added responsibility of working outside the home. Or perhaps you are a solo parent and are trying to be both mom and dad for your children, plus providing financially for the family.

Whatever your work situation, it's a fact that you have less time even to think about the summer—much less plan for sanity. No way will summertime be easy for you. The good news is that summer can be sane—but only if you plan!

FINDING SANITY TIME

The first step in planning for sanity is to assess your own situation. Do you work part time away from home? Are your hours flexible, or have you developed a home-based business that allows you to stay at home—at least physically? Are you employed full time outside the home? The latter is probably the toughest situation, so we'll start there—any of the other situations will just be easier!

Can you pull off a trio of extra vacation days this summer? Choose your favorite three Children's Days and plan to have one during each of the three months of summer. If you aren't able to do this, you can modify our suggestions for special weekends. The important thing is to give your children some individual time to do whatever they want to do.

Sometimes a happy day at home is as simple as inviting a friend over to play. Remember to make arrangements well in advance because of busy summer vacation schedules. Plan to pick the friend up in the morning and take him or her back right before supper. It helps peak the excitement level for your child if you plan all the things you are going to do while the friend is visiting. Include a lunch or snack picnic in the yard, an afternoon break to skate for an hour, and maybe a home movie with a cartoon from the library or a video tape for the television. Don't overplan. The kids will want time to do their own things.

Have a Home Vacation

Consider having a home vacation. If you begin the vacation mid-week, you can have a big family finale on the weekend and take advantage of a nearby vacation spot, like a water park. Maybe you live close to the beach or the mountains and can plan a side trip there. But the most important days are the ones before the weekend when you let your child either spend time with neighborhood friends or just have a few days at home to bum around.

Remember *why* you are doing this and keep your schedule free. Don't plan any housecleaning or special projects during these days. Make it clear that this time is for the child, and be available to jump in the car to go to the park or grab an ice-cream cone at a moment's notice.

Adapt a Backyard Circus

Why not adapt the backyard circus idea (see chapter 3) and make your child the star of the neighborhood for the day. Planning is half the fun and can be done on nights before the vacation starts. Send invitations to neighborhood friends and plan to pick up friends who are not within walking distance. If you plan the circus for late afternoon, working parents can usually arrange for you to pick up their children at day care, and they can retrieve them on their way home.

Don't forget the Clown Cupcakes and Paintbrush Cookies for the eats. Have the children wear circus clothes and bring their favorite wild animals (stuffed). You might also provide a box of "dress-up" clothes to add to the costumes.

Entertainment is provided by the "clowns" themselves—the children. Let them get in the center ring—made with a rope or garden hose. Provide a few props, and watch them perform.

Remember to have lots of balloons. You might even let the kids decorate them with colored markers. A white sheet for the kids to color and paint can be a special reminder of the day for your child. A cassette of happy circus music in the background adds a lot to the scene.

Mr. Roberts' Playbook (Berkley, $7.95) has several pages on how to make cages and animals out of simple materials. Or you can color paper plates with circus scenes and put them on a stick for a puppet show. Both are good souvenirs for the children to take home.

Cooking Up Fun!

Cooking days are fun for both boys and girls. Simple recipes for snacks and desserts can usually be handled with little supervision, but don't be afraid to let the children try "real" dishes. Learning to make biscuits is great. Making yeast bread is even better! And don't forget Aggression Cookies on page 28.

Your children will enjoy their special (at home) Children's Days with you. During the rest of the summer, why not plan a Children's Hour or supplement with a Super Saturday Children's Day?

"Just-Me-and-Mom" times don't have to take half a day. The point is to focus attention on each child. This may be sitting down for ten minutes to read a book together or letting one child help you prepare a microwave dinner and simple dessert.

For a special "Just-Me-and-Mom" time, arrange to have a sitter or friend pick up your child at day care and drop your son or daughter off for a lunch with mom. The money you pay the sitter will be well worth the message to your kid that he or she is special. Plus the lunch out will be a real treat.

Planning a VIP Office Visit

Depending on your work situation, consider letting your child spend a day (morning, afternoon, hour) at work with you. Explain your job and tell him/her all about what you do "at the office." Let your child ask questions and make a treat of an office tour. Introduce your children to your coworkers. Be sure to have your child's picture displayed on your desk, and if appropriate, display mementos from your child like notes, cards, and art work.

To accumulate some extra summer hours with your children, maybe you could go to work an hour early each day for a short span of time. The point is to evaluate your situation and grab all the time you can. It doesn't help you or your children to invest that time in taking a guilt trip. First, invest some time in planning your summer. You will want to go through the planning process outlined in Chapter 15. Just remember to be realistic. You may need to substitute "monthly" for "weekly" or "hour" for "morning." Instead of choosing four objectives, consider choosing two or even one. While you can't do everything, you can do something, and planning is the key.

Now that we have raised your "faith level," we are including a list of quick and easy suggestions for maximizing the time you can pull from your schedule to spend with your children.

SHORTCUTS TO SUMMERTIME SANITY
Cooking Tips

Since we all have to eat and most of us really enjoy it, we'll start with cooking tips.

- Homemade bread baking in the oven can make your home smell as if you've been slaving for hours in the kitchen. Simply buy frozen loaves and plop a loaf out to rise as you come in the door.
- You can adapt the dough for pizza fun with ready-grated cheeses and sliced pepperoni. Children love to help "make" their very own personal pizza!
- Another dough tip is to roll the dough out and brush with melted butter. Sprinkle with sugar and cinnamon, roll into a long roll, and cut with a thread. *Voilà!* You have homemade cinnamon rolls that will charm any family member!
- It's amazing what you can do with cookie dough you buy in rolls. Slice, bake, decorate with red hots or already prepared icing that you simply squeeze onto the cookies.
- Don't overlook the delicious frozen dinners. The variety available ten years ago known as TV dinners left much to be desired—basically flavor! Today's selection is much improved!

- One of our favorite quickies is Chinese take-out food. We set the table with flowers and candles, hide the paper containers, and presto! An Oriental dinner fit for a king or queen. Don't forget the fortune cookies and slices of oranges to top off your delicious meal.

Need Help? Play Fifty-two Pick-Up

No, we're not talking about the card game that you throw down fifty-two cards for some gullible person to pick up. This fifty-two pick-up might actually give you a little help!

Set a kitchen timer for fifty-two seconds. See how many items each child can pick up in that time:

- Yesterday's paper
- Umbrella at the back door
- Tennis racket
- Can of tennis balls (counts as three items)
- Wet towels (one point each)
- Dirty socks (one each if even number!)
- The last twelve issues of *Reader's Digest*
- Pair of shoes (two points)
- Dirty glasses
- Plate with half-eaten peanut butter sandwich (sorry! only one point)
- Half-empty can of soda

The winner is the person who gets closest to picking up fifty-two items.

For family fun at the dinner table, try changing places with one another. The family member must act like the person in whose chair he or she is sitting! This can be fun and quite revealing![3]

For other fun ideas of things you can do with little bits of time please refer to the Arps' trio of books, *60 One-Minute Family Builders, 60 One-Minute Memory Builders,* and *60 One-Minute Marriage Builders.* Remember, it doesn't take large blocks of time to build summertime sanity, but it does take some time. We hope that our suggestions will help you find it in the little places of your summertime schedule and that you will reap big results and lots of family fun.

CHAPTER 15

Your Summer Plans

The plans had been well laid; all was ready for Children's Day. We had planned an entire day at the zoo with two adults and both sets of our children. We had prepared a special lunch and driven the twenty miles to the zoo. Even the weather was cooperating—the sun was shining! Surely today would be a winner, right? *Wrong!*

Six children complained all day of being too hot and of having aching feet and too many mosquito bites. Everyone wanted to eat something other than the special food we had laboriously prepared. It was enough to make us want to give up our roles as mothers and prepare a sign: SIX CHILDREN FOR SALE—CHEAP! WILL THROW IN DOG, GUINEA PIGS, AND HAMSTERS FREE!

It's easy to get depressed and think that planning (and especially planning trips to the zoo) is the "pits." Perhaps the problem is that we live in a hasty society where we want instant everything—instant marriages, instant children, instant oatmeal, and instant sane summers!

Just because our plans are not "instantly" successful does *not* mean we should not plan. A sane, happy, productive summer takes planning *and* perseverance!

"The plans of the diligent lead surely to abundance, but every one who is hasty comes only to want" (Prov. 21:5, RSV). Too often, the word "diligence" is not even in our vocabulary! It's easier to procrastinate or to say planning takes too much time or to go the super-spiritual route and say, "If the Lord is leading us, we don't need to plan."

We've shared ideas with you for Children's Day and for "Just-Me-and-Mom" time. But since you won't be able to use every idea, how do *you* begin planning? We suggest that the best way is by planning to pray. You are not simply trying to fill up your summer schedule; you want to see something accomplished—to find God's best for your family this summer.

STEP 1: PLAN TO PRAY

We can make our plans, but the final outcome is in God's hands. Proverbs tells us that if we commit our work to the Lord, then it will succeed. Too many times we start planning not by praying, but by being "people watchers." When we try to pace ourselves by trying to keep up with the so-called "Super Moms," we are in immediate trouble! We begin to feel inadequate in our roles as mothers. Romans 12:3 instructs us to evaluate ourselves honestly—not to think too highly or too lowly, but to be realistic!

The summer our children were five and under, it was realistic to do very little because our energy level often registered below zero! We need to consider in our summer planning our own special situations, our husbands, our children, and our physical, emotional, and spiritual well-being. For instance, the working and/or single mom simply cannot plan as much to do as the mom who is basically home for the summer. The key is to allow ourselves to be stretched but to plan realistic goals. And we believe the best way to be a realistic planner is to begin by planning to pray!

Because we have on occasion (most occasions) been interrupted when we pray by a child, a husband, a dog, a cat, a telephone, a paper boy (you get the picture), we have sometimes gone alone to a park or a coffee shop or maybe a friend's house while she is away, to pray and plan our summer goals.

So first take the time at home or away to pray over your summers. Then plan realistically. And last, remember to persevere when the days get hot and humid!

Here are some tips for praying.

1. Allow yourself plenty of time so that you won't feel rushed (maybe two hours).

2. Get alone someplace where there will not be interruptions. Consider getting a sitter and going away to a quiet place.

3. Choose your best time of day. If you're a morning person, don't plan to get a lot done after the late show on TV.

4. Take a Bible, pen, and paper. A calender is also helpful—a *Priority Planner,* too!

5. Begin by reading some verses on planning. Some we suggest are:

Proverbs 3:5–6	Proverbs 21:5
Proverbs 16:1–3	Proverbs 24:3–4

6. List each child's strengths and weaknesses, and ask God to show you the areas to work on and to reinforce this summer. For an exercise to help you do this, please refer to Claudia Arp's *Almost 13*.

7. Write down your thoughts.

8. Thank God for what He is going to do in your family and through you this summer.

9. You're now ready to go on to Step 2.

STEP 2: PLAN TO PICK YOUR CHILDREN'S BRAINS

1. Why not set your children down and ask them what they would like to do this summer? We suggest making three lists.

> a. First, ask them, "What would you like to do this summer just for fun?"
>
> b. Second, ask, "What would you like to learn this summer?"
>
> c. Third, ask, "What would you like to do for others?"

2. Now look back through this book and take notes on ideas and suggestions you might like to use this summer. To help you, we have listed the various Children's Day activities we have shared with you, along with page references in a special index on page 189. Pick the ones that will help you meet your goals and objectives.

STEP 3: PLAN YOUR OBJECTIVES

After doing your research, you're ready to set objectives. Write out your objectives for the summer—custom-made around your own family's needs and interests. Maybe you will want to use objectives similar to those we set for our families.

- To develop a more personal relationship with my children.
- To improve communication with my children and to help them learn to express themselves better.
- To help my children develop a better self-image.
- To help my children develop responsibility and competence.
- To encourage my children to grow spiritually.
- To make travel time more enjoyable.

- To enrich my relationship with my husband.
- To develop as a person.

STEP 4: PLAN THE PROGRAM

Logically, the next thing to do is to ask ourselves, "*How* am I going to accomplish these objectives?"

For example, suppose one objective is to improve the communication with your Timmy the Turtle, who usually stays in his shell. How can you help Tim communicate better? The answer to that question will yield a series of activities necessary for the accomplishment of this objective. (With Tim it might be as simple as spending time alone together and using questions and games to draw him out.)

In this step you are listing the sequence of events necessary to get you from where you are to where you want to be (from silence and an occasional "yeah" to the point where you wish Timmy would be quiet!).

Let's give an example.

Summer Objective: To develop a more intimate and personal relationship with our child.

Possible Activities:

1. Have a special time each week with child alone.

2. Work through a communication project together this summer.

3. Make something together with the child that he/she wants to make.

4. Take a shopping trip alone with child to buy supplies for school for fall.

When you have written out your objectives and have your list all made, then you can go on to Step 5.

STEP 5: PLAN YOUR SUMMER SCHEDULE

The list of activities may become rather lengthy as you anticipate accomplishing all your objectives for the summer. So you are now faced with the problem of arranging and working them all in. Since adding ten hours to each day isn't a possibility, what do you do now?

We've found it helps to plan the ideas by month and week. Seeing the schedule on paper helps us see how it all goes together.

In order to schedule your summer, we suggest you purchase a copy of Linda Dillow's *Priority Planner*. While any planning calendar will do, we will be developing a sample summer schedule around pages from this planner.

In this step you get down to the practical. If you have listed too many activities, you must pick and choose the projects you want to tackle this summer. To begin doing this, list the activities in order of priority, and start by scheduling the ones you consider most important.

What follows is one mother's Sample Summer Schedule. She has two children—Jeff, age ten, and Jenny, age six. You may choose to plan more or fewer activities and be more or less specific than this mom. This sample schedule is only given to help you see the process on paper.

SAMPLE SUMMER SCHEDULE

Objective #1—To develop a more personal relationship with my children.

Possible Activities	*Estimated Time Needed*
1. Children's Day—Backyard Circus for Jenny. Jeff helps as my attendant.	2 days
2. Jeff—"Just-Me-and-Mom" hike in the woods	1 morning
3. Jeff and Jenny—Pool Picnic—Children's Day	1 day

Objective #2—To improve communication with my children and to help them learn to express themselves better.

Possible Activities	*Estimated Time Needed*
1. Children's Day—Making Puppets	1 morning
2. Jeff—"Just-Me-and-Mom" communication lunch	2 hours
3. Jenny—Communication lunch	2 hours

Objective #3—To help my children develop a better self-image.

Possible Activities	*Estimated Time Needed*
1. Children's Day—Inner beauty/Outer beauty	½ day
2. Special Person Party for Dad	1 day and evening
3. Jeff—Go through *My Family, Myself*	15–30 minutes a week
4. Jenny—Go through *My Book about Me*	15–30 minutes a week

Objective #4—To help my children develop responsibility and competence.

Possible Activities	Estimated Time Needed
1. Children's Day—Work on writing skills	½ day
2. Jeff—Make dinner	1 hour
3. Jenny—Make Raggedy Ann Lunch with Mom	1 hour
4. Weekly summer charts	

Objective #5—To encourage my children to grow spiritually.

Possible Activities	Estimated Time Needed
1. Jeff—Make a Proverbs notebook	15 minutes daily for one month
2. Jenny—Read through *Muffin Book*	15 minutes three times a week
3. Children's Day—Send a missionary box	1 day

Objective #6—To make travel time more enjoyable.

Possible Activities	Estimated Time Needed
1. Children's Day—Make Travel Notebooks	½ day
2. Mom's Bag assembly	1 day

Objective #7—To enrich my relationship with my husband.

Possible Activities	Estimated Time Needed
1. Make coupon book	1 hour
2. Two dates per month with Dad	6 evenings
3. Weekend away	one weekend

Objective #8—To develop as a person.

Possible Activities	Estimated Time Needed
1. Bible study on tongue from Proverbs	15 minutes a day
2. Tennis lessons and lunch out	1 day a week

Now that this mom has her summer schedule planned, she transfers the activities onto her monthly calendar (p. 158). Then each week she writes the week's activities in her *Priority Planner* (p. 157).

We began this chapter by saying that a sane, happy, and productive summer does not just happen—it takes planning and perseverance. Now you've planned your summer schedule for sanity and are ready to enjoy a fun-filled summer with your family. Before beginning your summer, however, consider planning for one more thing—a healthy response to summer disasters.

Priorities/ Week of

1 LORD • *"But seek first His kingdom and His righteousness; and all these things shall be added to you."* **Matt. 6:33**

2 HUSBAND • *"An excellent wife is the crown of her husband..."* **Prov. 12:4**

3 CHILDREN • *"Behold, children are a gift of the Lord."* **Psalm 127:3**

4 HOME • *"She looks well to the ways of her household, and does not eat the bread of idleness."* **Prov. 31:27**

5 YOURSELF • *"You shall love your neighbor as yourself."* **Matt. 19:19**

6 OUTSIDE THE HOME • *"Go therefore and make disciples of all nations..."* **Matt. 28:19**

Things To Do This Week

Weekly Schedule

Monday

Communication lunch with Jenny

Tuesday

Wednesday

Children's Day
morning: make puppets
afternoon: pool

Thursday

Make "Dads Coupon Book"!

Friday

Mom's Day!

Saturday

Date with Dad!

Sunday

157

MY SUMMER PLAN

JUNE

Theme Communication
- M Communication Lunch - Jenny
- TU
- W C.O. Puppets - Morning
- TH Make "Dad's" Coupon Book! Pool - Afternoon
- F Mom's Day!
- SA Date with Dad!
- SU

Theme Communication
- M Communication Breakfast - Jeff
- TU
- W C.O. Trip to the Zoo!
- TH
- F Mom's Day!
- SA
- SU

Theme Responsibility
- M Jeff and Mom make Dinner.
- TU Morning - Writing Day
- W C.O. Afternoon - Nature Hike
- TH
- F Mom's Day!
- SA Jenny and Mom make Lunch!
- SU Date with Dad!

Theme Travel
- M Assemble Bags!
- TU
- W C.O. Travel Notebooks - and then Pool!
- TH
- F Mom's Day!
- SA
- SU

JULY

Theme
- M
- TU
- W Family Vacation to Afar
- TH
- F Time for Fun in the Car!
- SA
- SU

Theme
- M
- TU
- W
- TH
- F
- SA
- SU

Theme Relationship
- M Mom and Jeff - Ice Cream
- TU
- W C.O. Back Yard Circus Day!
- TH
- F Mom's Day!
- SA Date with Dad!
- SU

Theme Relationship
- M Mom and Jenny - Ice Cream
- TU
- W C.O. Back Yard Circus Day.2
- TH
- F Mom's Day!
- SA
- SU

AUGUST

Theme Spiritual
- M Jeff - Make Proverbs Notebook
- TU
- W C.O. - Make Missionary Box
- TH
- F Mom's Day!
- SA
- SU

Theme Self Image
- M
- TU
- W C.O. Inner-Outer Beauty Secret Pals Drawing
- TH
- F Mom's Day!
- SA Weekend Away With Dad Alone
- SU

Theme Self Image
- M School Shopping Trip - Jeff
- TU
- W C.O. Plan "Special Person Party for Dad"
- TH
- F Mom's Day!
- SA Date with Dad!
- SU

Theme Relationship
- M School Shopping Trip - Jenny
- TU
- W C.O. Last Fling at Pool!
- TH
- F Mom's Day!
- SA
- SU

CHAPTER 16

Disasters Turned to Delight

Birthdays were fast approaching, and much thought had been given concerning gifts for Jarrett and Joel, whose birthdays are a week apart. After much deliberation it was decided to give the boys a Ping-Pong table. The three Arp boys shared a large room, and with a little rearranging there would be plenty of room for a Ping-Pong table and many hours of fun. Claudia spent a lot of time planning a new room arrangement, and at last she was ready to start moving furniture.

The big day arrived, and the Ping-Pong table was delivered. But there was a problem: the table, even unassembled, would *not* go down the circular stairs to the boys' room. After two hours of pushing, shoving, and praying, it became obvious. *No way would that Ping-Pong table go down those stairs!*

There was no game room or basement, and the car had to go in the garage. And to top it all off, the table had been badly scratched in the attempts to get it down the stairs, so it could not be returned to the store. What a bummer! Claudia had spent much time, thought, and money to make her boys' birthdays special, and it wasn't turning out at all the way she had planned!

You try to do the right thing and it's a disaster. Is it really worth trying?

Disasters know no season. They especially like to appear on special days like birthdays and anniversaries. One such anniversary disaster has come to be known as the "Dillow Flood."

"After trying unsuccessfully for six months to get away alone," Linda relates, "Jody and I were finally escaping, and for four whole days we'd be minus children and telephone. Our plan was to drive to the mountains of Arkansas and spend our anniversary camping by the lovely and peaceful Missouri River. Visions of the woods, seclusion, birds singing, books, hikes, laughter, and loving filled my mind. I was ready for this!

"There was just enough time to run to the store and splurge on thick steaks and lots of bacon before we left. Excitedly, I drove home and carried the steaks into the house, shouting, 'Honey, let's go!' But instead of a husband ready to travel, I encountered several neighbors mopping water into pails. There was water everywhere—all over my carpeting, which now gave a 'slush-slush' sound when I walked. Jody had decided to fix the leaky faucet in the bathroom.

"So instead of a romantic evening with my husband, walking by the river, I vacuumed water from everywhere, pulled up wall-to-wall carpeting, hung it over the fence in the back yard to dry, and then prayed it wouldn't rain and soak everything again!

"As if this wasn't enough to spoil our anniversary, while moving our bedroom furniture to get the carpet up I lost my wedding ring. So instead of a romantic evening with my husband, I spent our anniversary with tears streaming down my face, flashlight in hand, searching in every nook and cranny of the house for my wedding ring!"

It just doesn't seem fair!

"WHY ME, LORD?"

We wish we could promise that if you seek this summer to be all God wants you to be as a parent, a spouse, and a Christian, that every Children's Day will be warm and sunny, every child cheerful and obedient, every mate loving and helpful, and every circumstance perfect—and that no sickness, broken-down cars, monster Ping-Pong tables, or floods will darken the door of your home!

But we have no magic "disaster preventer" spray, nor do we have a perfect batting record of right responses to trials. More than once we've been known to slip quietly into the bathroom, have a good cry, and ask, "Why me, Lord?"

Trials might be easier to accept if we knew *why* the Ping-Pong table got stuck in the staircase or the carpets got soggy! God doesn't promise always to tell us why, but He *does* promise us that there is a purpose in trials. Often, character is built through the failures and disasters of our lives. In Romans 5:3-4 we see that our trials can have a real purpose and can actually benefit us:

We can rejoice, too, when we run into problems and trials for we know that they are good for us—they help us learn to be patient. And patience develops strength of character in us and helps us trust God more each time we use it until finally our hope and faith are strong and steady. (Rom. 5:3–4, TLB)

Do you see the word in this passage that is exactly what all of us "less than Super Moms" need? It starts with a *p—patience!* It's what we thought we had until we had children! Patience is not learned when everything is rosy, but in the trials and struggles, the Ping-Pong tables and the floods of life. When the zoo trip is the "pits," then patience is learned. And strength of character and trust in God are results of patience. If our hope in life is to be strong and steady in our faith in Christ, then there *is* a real purpose in trials. Also, in Romans 8:28 God promises to work all things for good in our lives if we put our trust in Him. How can we demonstrate trust in God? By giving Him thanks in all things.

HOW DO YOU SAY "THANK YOU"?

In 1 Thessalonians 5:18 we read, "In everything give thanks; for this is God's will for you in Christ Jesus." You may be wondering, "But what about the broken ankle, the ruined day, the plans that failed? How can I possibly feel thankful about these disasters?"

The verse does not say we must "feel thankful," but rather it says "give thanks." There is a huge difference! Some summer days you may be grateful for your children and *feel* thankful to be a mother. On other summer days you don't feel anything about being a mother except "blah." You're hot, the children have spilled lemonade on the clean floor, and the dog has tracked it all over the house. Everything is sticky! At times like this, if you're like us, you will have no feelings of thankfulness concerning motherhood and sticky floors.

On days like these our attitude of thankfulness is based on a decision, an act of will, not feelings. When we decide to thank God in a situation we don't feel thankful in or don't even understand, we are demonstrating that we have chosen to trust God in this situation, that we acknowledge that He is in control, and that we believe His promise to work this situation for our good.

BIG AND LITTLE PACKAGES

Trials come in all sizes. The Ping-Pong table was a *big* thing and a *big* disaster. The flood was a *big* mess! These big trials are difficult to accept, and yet sometimes the smaller trials—the grating, irritating ones that appear daily—seem harder to deal with. The children are arguing *again,* the expensive roast did a shrinking act, the husband is late for dinner *again* (and no phone call), and there are footprints on the freshly waxed floor.

WE CAN CHOOSE

Trials *will* come this summer, and *now* is the time to decide how you will respond to the next disaster at your house. Remember:

1. There *is* a purpose in trials (see Rom. 5:3–4).

2. God promises to work all things together for good for those who love Him (see Rom. 8:28).

3. Our response should be to give thanks and to trust (see 1 Thess. 5:18).

We all must make choices. When a child doesn't want "Just-Me-and-Mom" time, when no one likes your "crafty" idea for Children's Day, when your mate has no time for a date with you, when your well-laid plans have been canceled, you have a choice:

1. You can give up and decide it's not worth it.

2. You can fight against God, your husband, your children, yourself, the air conditioner, or whoever or whatever isn't "working right."

3. You can respond God's way—thank Him, trust Him to work it together for good, and see God's purposes of patience, character, and hope working in your life.

But what about those times when we don't react the right way?

One more very important thing God promises is that He forgives! When we blow it, He forgives when we ask (see 1 John 1:9). And He wants us to forgive ourselves and change the wrong reaction into a right response. Just because we initially blow it does not mean we have to follow a wrong reaction with a wrong response. *It's never too late to make the right choice and go God's way!*

Back to the Ping-Pong Table

Let's go back to the six-by-twelve-foot monster stuck in the circular staircase. Claudia's first reaction was *not* "Oh, goody, a Ping-Pong table stuck in the staircase! What fun!" But she decided as a choice of her will not to be depressed, but to thank God and ask Him for an alternative.

Since returning the table to the store was not an option, what other possibilities were open to the Arps? They could try to sell it or give it away or just put it in the storage room and write it off as a bad scene. *Or* . . . if Mom was flexible enough, it just might fit in the living room. (Isn't it every woman's dream to have a Ping-Pong table decorate her living room?)

Fortunately, they had selected a table that folded up easily and could be rolled into the hall when not in use. So Mom decided to thank God and flex. If they wanted to be able to play Ping-Pong as a family, they couldn't wait until the next move to the next house or until they were rich enough to build a game room. It had to be now. Now was the time to say, "It doesn't fit at all with our living room decor, but thank You, Lord, that we have a large living room and that with a little moving and shoving we can play Ping-Pong as a family."

For those years the table was up about half the time, so half of the time it was quite obvious that the Arps were raising boys and not competing for a "House Beautiful" award. Does Claudia know why this trial came their way? Not really, but God says through proper response to trials He works patience, character, and hope into our lives. That's not something we can measure, but it is an encouragement to us to know that God is at work in the midst of unwanted circumstances.

Of Carpets and Rings

Now let's go back to Linda's ruined anniversary . . . the soggy carpets, the lost wedding ring, the romantic vacation forgotten. Forgotten, that is, by Linda!

The next day Jody made an incredible suggestion: "Honey, let's forget about the carpets and the wedding ring and head for the Arkansas mountains."

"You've got to be kidding!" she said. "The house is in utter chaos, the carpet is hanging over the fence, and I feel unmarried without my ring!" By this time, a romantic walk by the river was the last thing she wanted. She would rather have stayed home, dried the carpets, put the house in order, and found the wedding ring.

But they did make the trip. During the five-hour drive to the mountains Linda prayed repeatedly, "Lord, You know how crummy I feel. I don't want to be alone with Jody, but I choose in my will to thank You in the midst of the flood, my lost wedding ring, and our spoiled anniversary. I choose to forget all of this and concentrate on loving my husband. I don't feel like it, but I choose this because I know it's Your will."

"My wedding ring was never found and my carpets were lumpy in places, but the Dillow disaster was turned into a delight. Jody and I had the most wonderful time together—such close and special conversations and even a romantic walk by the river! I believe God gave us those special days together because I chose to turn my wrong reaction into a right response."

WHAT IS YOUR CHOICE?

You've planned for many things this summer—fun times, growing times, opportunities for loving. The one thing you have *not* planned into your summers is disasters! But they arrive anyway.

Disasters take no planning, but your *responses* to them do! *Now* is the time to decide how you will respond when the lemonade is spilled or the carpet is soggy. Will you be angry at God, or will you choose to thank Him and trust Him in the midst of your trial?

With the right response to trials it is possible to turn our disasters to delight, as we see in this poem Claudia wrote on a real "disaster day."

Disasters

What do you do with a disaster?
Just put up a new coat of plaster?
Or a quick veneer of paint
And continue to look like a saint?

What do you do with three boys
Who usually are such joys?
But on this day they can't seem to play
Together or with friends in a peaceful way.

What do you do when you're ready for dinner
And Mom has fixed what she thinks is a winner—
And all she hears for her work of an hour
Is "*ugh*. This pie is just too sour!"?

What about when a water balloon you're told
Hit a lady and was much too cold?
You know this wasn't done by your dear
But find he's guilty when the facts are clear.

What do you do when you're all trying to share
With one of your friends that Jesus does care—
But all that he hears is the way you act?
You try to press forward but you only go back!

What about those times when it's an uphill fight
And even when trying things don't go right?

164

The hard times as the good times are all a part
Of living with Jesus in your home and your heart.

We all make mistakes. We all can be wrong.
But remember don't let it go on for too long.
The quicker we come together and say,
"Forgive us, dear Lord, we've gone the wrong way—
Take back control of our lives, we pray,
And help our family have a better day,"
The quicker our friend who needs Jesus can see
That Jesus is just as real as real can be!

He loves us not only just when we're good
But also the times we're not like we should.
So when at your house a disaster strikes
Don't give up on those little "tykes."

Just talk to the Lord and ask Him today
To shed His light upon your way—
Then you'll find the joy that Jesus can give
In your heart and home will continue to live!

CHAPTER 17

Be a Memory Maker

Now as you end this book and begin your summers, take an imaginary jump into the fall and reflect back. What will have been accomplished? What new skills learned? Objectives reached? Projects completed (or partially completed)? How many triumphant hours will you have logged in your cars? All these many hours together as a family will be memories in September. They will lock us together as a unique family unit. We can pull them out and enjoy them in the cold of winter.

Family memories are one of our most priceless possessions, and summer is a great time for adding to our treasure chest. Memories help give us a sense of identity in a world full of people crying out, "Who am I?" Shared memories give us a sense of belonging and are ours for keeping! No one possesses the same set of memories that we have in our family or you do in yours. What makes your family unique? All your shared experiences. A family should be a composite of memories—shared moments revisited that pull us closer together. Sadly, in our individualistic society today families are often a composite of individuals, each going separate ways—dinner alone in front of the TV, vacations alone at summer camp.

How can we change this picture? As we walk through our summers, how can we maximize the memory-building potential of each new experience? What can we do to preserve and create memories instead of simply allowing life to drift by?

"I REMEMBER"

Sometimes creative ideas for memory building originate through sheer desperation. One mom found herself traveling alone with three small children. Their international flight had been turned back in the middle of the night. After a sleepless night this young mother spent a whole day on a bus touring New York City with her children. At last they were at the airport once again. The children were exhausted, Mom was super exhausted, and there was still an hour before boarding time. Mom's Bag was empty, Children's Bags were empty, and they were too tired for snacks. A belief that God would help in this desperate situation, and a request to Him for wisdom and creativity, resulted in the game of "I Remember!"

Each thought back on the day's bus tour of New York City and tried to remember everything possible. They took turns and tried to see who could continue the longest remembering things and places they had seen. Before they had finished it was time to board. This little game helped them remember and catalog the things they had seen and left a positive impression of what otherwise could have been remembered as a real "disaster day."

CHECK YOUR ARCHIVES

One definition of memories is that they are glad moments preserved in the archives of our minds. Dig into your "archives" and remember your most vivid memories from childhood.

We asked several friends, "What do you remember from childhood?" Among the answers were fun times fishing with the family, visiting Grandmother, making special Christmas decorations as a family, having lunch alone with Mom, and catching octopi at the seashore. Tragically, one friend's most vivid memory was of her sixth birthday. She was taking apart the doll her parents had given her, all the while watching with bitter disappointment as they left on a trip. When we asked our "funny friend" what she remembered from her childhood, she said "I'm still in it!" (she just turned forty!).

We are sobered when we think of the potential we have—to build either positive or negative memories for our children. Our desire for you is that this coming summer would be a positive time of adding to your children's memory storehouses. Many treasured memories are from summertime when families vacation and there is more opportunity for "togetherness." Why not gather your children together and take your own "memory inventory"? Discover your children's best memories from last summer.

Family or Furniture?

We must often examine our priorities. Which comes first—people or possessions? Family or furniture?

Claudia tells about a special family vacation.

"A few years ago while living in Germany we made plans to go to the Scandinavian countries for a family vacation. Many hours were spent in budgeting and planning for this vacation. As we made ferry reservations, we were surprised at the high cost of getting a car and five Arps from Germany to Norway.

"That money could be used in many other ways. Should we spend *that* much on a family vacation? After all, we really could use some new clothes, maybe even a new couch. As we think back, the clothes would have worn out by now (or been out of style!) and the old couch 'recovered' is still as comfy as ever.

"But the shared memories of those two weeks together have no price tag—cold shrimp fresh from the shrimp boats in Oslo, eaten in the rain . . . the train ride to Bergan and how God provided a perfect place to stay when there were 'no rooms in the inn' (or at least no cheap ones) . . . the Viking ships . . . the sandy beaches in Sweden . . . the long hours in the car as Jarrett learned his multiplication tables. . . .

"Castles and long conversations . . . times uniquely shared together as a family building strong bonds for the future. Yes, those big special times are worth it!"

Cataloging Memories

One way the Arp family has kept their vacation memories alive is through pictures. As we think back on our childhood, the most vivid memories are those scenes we viewed over and over in pictures, snapshots, slides, home movies, and tapes. They enable us to relive that winning soccer game, that special Children's Day, that family vacation, and they help catalog our summer memories for our families. Each summer adventure comes alive again as we view it! *Nothing* is as interesting to a child as seeing himself/herself from the incubator to the present by means of pictures.

Too often we catalog with pictures but neglect the taping. Our families have laughed until we cried listening to fifteen-year-old recordings of the children! Making "tape letters" for grandparents and friends is our way of preserving treasured recordings. It's easy to promise yourself each year that you'll make a tape of the children, but we found it got done only when we told Grandmother to expect a tape. Then we were committed! After grandparents listened and laughed, they sent the tape back for us to keep.

Refrigerator Memories

Over the years the Arps' refrigerator became their communication center and catchall for latest cartoons, snapshots, interesting articles, and notes. When new items replaced outdated ones, Claudia simply stuffed the old ones in a drawer by the refrigerator.

One day, when the drawer would no longer close, she decided to make a Refrigerator Memories Scrapbook. It took no organizational ability and is just a hodge-podge collection of memories—fun to pull out on a rainy summer evening and remember how fast the years passed by.

Make a "Roots" Book

One mother of four boys took cataloging memories a step beyond slides and tapes by developing the family's own "Roots" book. She kept a book that recorded funny sayings of the children, family happenings, interesting news of friends and relatives, and other special events for sixteen years! She said it never failed to entertain them as they read about:

- Marty, who at five seriously thought he could fly and designed elaborate costumes for that attempt.
- Marshall, who made up the most fascinating lyrics and once slept in the dentist chair . . . through three fillings!
- the logical comments of Mitch, who announced: "I can tie my shoes, bounce the basketball under my knees, and even blow my nose. I must be six instead of four."[1]

Most of us haven't kept a "Roots" book for sixteen years, but we can begin now. It's never too late to begin cataloging memories!

Why not begin your own "Roots" book one Children's Day this summer? A scrapbook, a fancy book, or an old notebook will do. Assemble several pens, pencils, stickers, and creative minds. Ask each child to write down all the clever, ridiculous, happy, and disastrous things they can remember about themselves. Then, ask them to do the same thing for the other family members. Compile the best selections in your "Roots" book, adding appropriate art work or stickers.

DOING IT YOUR WAY

Cataloging memories is one way to remember the special family times of togetherness. Building traditions is another. One definition of tradition is "an activity that sets us apart in order to bring us together."

A friend of ours recently reminded us of the link between traditions and memories. Her point was that although our children may not have geographical roots, the richness of tradition in our homes can give them a deep sense of belonging no matter where we live. For many families life is different from the way it was fifty years ago. There are few grandmothers, aunts, and uncles nearby and no town where they live from birth to death. Our whole society is constantly on the move! More than ever, we feel the need today for strong family traditions, special ways we do things as a family over and over again.

James Dobson says it like this: "Traditions have an important role in giving a family a sense of cohesiveness and stability. Involved is how the family sees itself. I'm referring to those family events that are done the same way every year and are anticipated as a time of love, closeness, friendship, and fellowship between family members."[2]

MAKING BIRTHDAY MEMORIES

Many family traditions cluster around birthdays and Christmas. Menu planning is a Dillow birthday tradition. The birthday person plans the menu for the entire day. So on Mom's and Dad's birthdays the meals are expensive and elegant. And on the children's birthdays the meals were—you guessed it—*junky!* For example, on Tommy's birthday, his menu choices were pancakes for breakfast; pizza for lunch; hamburgers, French fries, and milkshakes for dinner. But what fun Tommy had planning his own special meals! The children got so excited about having what *they* wanted to eat that the menu was usually planned weeks in advance.

A friend shared this special birthday tradition: "Our most important gift to our birthday child is prayer because it is an investment into his life for eternity. On the birthday morning, my husband and I rise an hour earlier to pray specifically for the child. We pray for his future, his mate, his education, his friends, his growth in Christ, and his character. We also read together passages of Scripture. That hour passes very quickly, and the day begins with a bubble of joy in our hearts."

CREATING CHRISTMAS MEMORIES

Another family's Christmas tradition involves nightgowns! Each year Grandmother makes "all the same" nightgowns for the women and girls in the family. What a special memory—lovely new nightgowns every Christmas, their similarity binding each woman and girl into the family.

Linda shares, "My frustration at Christmas time had been that the gifts were so exciting that they seemed to overshadow God's gift. So years ago we began having a Christmas Eve birthday party for Jesus. It began with a special dinner and *always* a chocolate pound cake for the birthday cake. We sang "Happy Birthday" to Jesus and talked about what we wanted to give to Him. Then we decided on a private gift, something of ourselves to give to Him. We wrote it on a piece of paper and tied it to the Christmas tree. After dinner we lit the lights on the tree, turned out the other lights, and prayed together as a family. This tradition helped bring the true meaning of Christmas on Christmas Eve before the presents on Christmas morning!"

As the children grew older, singing happy birthday to Jesus was definitely not on their "cool" list of things to do. The Dillows continued to have a special Christmas Eve dinner, to pray together as a family for the goals each family member has for the new year, and to celebrate together. Traditions change as our families change, but we continue to make memories.

CREATING SUMMER MEMORIES

Perhaps you already have family traditions for birthdays and Christmas. But what about the summer? What can you do to insure that this summer will be a time of building family traditions—memories that will last a lifetime?

Some traditions "just happened"—like the birthday menus. There are probably things that your family "always" does the same way. Be glad and preserve those "just-happened" traditions. But at the same time, consider *creating* summer traditions!

In our homes we created the traditions of a planned summer—of Children's Day, "Just-Me-and-Mom" times, summer dates with Dad, and a summer project for Mom. In years to come, we want our children to remember that fun backyard circus, the Aggression Cookies they pounded to bits, being king for a day at a Special Person Party, anticipating the treasure from Mom's Surprise Bag, and those special times of coupon cashing.

Years down the road we can see our children planning Children's Day and "Just-Me-and-Mom" times with their children. Someday maybe our children will guide their own children into the wonderful world of teenagehood through the Teenage Challenge tradition!

Summer traditions—summer memories, yours for keeping, yours for treasuring, yours for sharing, yours for passing down to future generations, yours for creating summer sanity!

Now is the time to begin, for

The day will come!

Much sooner than we think—
When there will be no dripping bathing suits and
    towels on the bathroom floors—
No extra traffic of little feet on our freshly
    vacuumed carpets.
The music will not be blaring
There will be no slammed doors—
The milk carton will not be left beside the cookie
    crumbs on the kitchen table.

Children's Day will be a memory
"Just-Me-and-Mom" times will be a thing of the
    past
No more hectic days in the car—
Gone will be those opportunities to listen, laugh,
    and love with a child . . .
To lead them to new truths about God, love, and
    life.
Gone are the opportunities to teach the joy of giving
    ourselves to others.

No, those unique opportunities will be gone.
Our homes will once again be in order.
All will be quiet.
Perhaps as we look at our orderly houses we might
    like to trip over a toy fire truck
Or see the garage lights left burning once again.
To have one more chance to build and encourage, to
    plan one more Children's Day or go on one more
    "date with Mom."

But it will be too late . . .
Our job with the special children God has entrusted
    to us will be done.
Now is all the time we have . . .
    Today . . .
        Tomorrow . . .
            These coming three months . . .
Now is the time for building for the future . . .

    Now is the time for

SANITY IN THE SUMMERTIME![3]

Appendix I

A STUDY OF PROVERBS—TRAPS TO AVOID

Subject & Verses	God's View	My commitment or decision is:
1. Losing Temper Proverbs 14:17, 29 18:2, 6–7 19:19 20:3 22:24–25		
2. Laziness Proverbs 10:26 12:11, 24 13:4 16:26 19:15, 24 20:4, 13 22:13 24:30–34		
3. Wrong Use of Tongue Proverbs 10:19, 21 11:12–13 13:2–3 15:1, 4, 23–28 18:8, 21		
4. Pride Proverbs 11:2 13:10		

16:5, 18
18:12

5. Disobeying Parents
Proverbs 13:1
15:5

6. Wrong Planning or No Planning
Proverbs 13:16, 19
15:22
16:9
24:3–4, 6, 8

7. Rejecting Criticism
Proverbs 13:18
15:31–32
17:10
23:12

8. Unwise Use of Money
Proverbs 21:20

9. Lying
Proverbs 14:5
19:9

10. Jealousy
Proverbs 14:30

11. Cheating
Proverbs 20:10, 17, 23

12. Rebellion
Proverbs 22:1–5

TEENAGE CHALLENGE
CODE OF CONDUCT STUDY

I. Obedience—Disobedience

1. To whom are we to be obedient?

    A. Ephesians 6:1, Colossians 3:20 _____

    _____

B. Hebrews 13:17 _____

_____

C. Deuteronomy 6:17 _____

_____

2. What does the Bible instruct us to do concerning all those in authority over us?

1 Timothy 2:1–4 _____

_____

Romans 13:1–7 _____

_____

3. What is the one exception in being obedient to those in authority? Acts 5:17–32 _____

_____

What would be an example of this today? _____

_____

4. What is *your commitment* to the above principles for your teenage years?

I will be obedient to:	YES	NO
My parents (to all rules and what my parents request)		
To teachers and school authorities		
To others in authority over me		

II. Respect (Honor)—Disrespect (Dishonor)

1. Whom are we to honor and respect?

Exodus 20:12; Ephesians 6:2; Matthew 15:4 _____

_____

John 5:23; Proverbs 3:9; 1 Timothy 6:13–16 _____

_____

Romans 12:10–14 _____

_____

Leviticus 19:32; 1 Timothy 5:3 _____

_____

1 Timothy 6:1–2; 1 Peter 2:18 _____

_____

1 Peter 3:7 _____

1 Peter 2:17 _____

Romans 12:17 _____

2. How can we show honor or respect to others?

2 Timothy 2:21–24 _____

_____

Romans 2:9–11 _____

John 12:26 _____

Proverbs 15:33; 18:12; 29:23 _____

Proverbs 20:3 _____

3. How do we show dishonor (or disrespect)?

Romans 1:21–24 _____

_____

Romans 2:23 _____

_____

4. Who gives honor? John 5:44; 2 Peter 1:17; Psalm 15:1–4 _____

_____

5. What is *your commitment* to the above principles for your teenage years?

I choose to honor and respect in my words, actions, and attitudes:	YES	NO
My parents		
All adults		
My teachers (even when I disagree with them!)		
Property of others		
The rights of others		
In these ways I will show respect and honor for God		

III. Honesty (Truthfulness)—Dishonesty (Lying)

1. What should our heart attitude be towards telling the truth?

   1 Corinthians 13:6 _____

   Psalm 51:6 _____

   Proverbs 23:23 _____

   Proverbs 13:5 _____

2. What commands does God give us concerning truthfulness?

   Ephesians 4:15, 25 _____

   _____

   Colossians 3:9 _____

   Ephesians 6:14 _____

   _____

3. What are some benefits of telling the truth?

   Psalm 15:1–5 _____

   John 8:32 _____

   John 18:37 _____

   Proverbs 12:17–19 _____

   _____

4. What is God's view of lying?

   Proverbs 12:22 _____

   Proverbs 6:16–19 _____

5. What are some of the results of not telling the truth?

   Psalm 31:18 _____

   Psalm 12:2–4 _____

   Psalm 59:12–15 _____

   Proverbs 26:27–28 _____

   Proverbs 21:6 _____

   Isaiah 59:12–15 _____

   _____

6. How can you avoid dishonesty?

   Proverbs 10:18–19 _____

Proverbs 13:5 _____

Ephesians 4:25 _____

Philippians 4:8 _____

_____

_____

7. Scripture to memorize to help in this area:

   Psalm 39:1 _____

   _____

   Psalm 119:29 _____

   _____

   Psalm 119:163 _____

   _____

8. What is *your commitment* to the above principles for your teenage years?

I will:	YES	NO
Speak the truth		
Let my yes be yes and my no be no		
Not speak half-truths or part of truth		
Not be deceptive to my parents or others		

IV. Responsibility (Faithfulness)—Irresponsibility (Faithlessness)

1. What are the benefits of developing faithfulness and responsibility?

   Proverbs 28:20 _____

   Psalm 101:6; 31:23 _____

   _____

   Luke 19:12–17 _____

   _____

   2 Timothy 2:2 _____

   Proverbs 20:6–7 _____

2. Why should we be faithful and responsible in our work? (Chores, school work, jobs, etc.)

Psalm 62:12 _____

Ecclesiastes 5:12 _____

2 Thessalonians 3:10 _____

_____

Matthew 5:16 _____

3. What should our attitude be toward work?

Nehemiah 4:6 _____

Proverbs 16:3 _____

Luke 5:5 _____

Colossians 3:23–4 _____

4. What is our goal in working?

John 6:27 _____

_____

5. What is God's view (and/or the results) of irresponsibility and laziness?

Proverbs 10:26 _____

Proverbs 12:11, 24 _____

_____

Proverbs 13:4 _____

Proverbs 24:30–34 _____

_____

6. What is *your commitment* to the above principles for your teenage years?

I commit myself to:	YES	NO
Carry out all tasks (at home, school, etc.) with high standards		
Behave or respond according to rules and standards even when no one is around		
Complete all tasks		

V. Spirit of Rejoicing—Moodiness/Grumpiness

1. What attitude should we have when faced with problems and trials?

   Romans 5:3–5 _____

   _____

   Philippians 2:5–11 _____

   _____

   Philippians 4:4–7, 11 _____

   _____

2. How can we develop a spirit of rejoicing?

   1 Thessalonians 5:16–18 _____

   _____

   Romans 8:26–28 _____

   _____

   Philippians 4:8–9 _____

   _____

3. What is *your commitment* to the above principles for your teenage years?

I will:	YES	NO
Not allow circumstances to change my moods		
Be happy in my heart, rejoice		
Give thanks in all situations		

SUMMARY
CODE OF CONDUCT BIBLE STUDY

Obedience
   To all rules and what my parents say
   Complete and right away

Respect
   To all adults
   To authority
   To property
   To rights of others

Honesty
> Yes is yes, no is no
> Speak the truth
> No deceiving, or half-truths, or part of truth

Responsibility
> Carry out all tasks to high standard
> Behave or respond according to rules or standards when no one is
>   around
> Complete all tasks

Spirit of Rejoicing
> Not allow circumstances to change my moods
> Be happy in heart—rejoicing—thankful

Appendix II

A TOPICAL APPROACH TO FAMILY LIVING FROM PROVERBS[1]

The Power of Our Words

11:9	18:21
12:18	25:11
15:4	
18:8	

The Source of Our Words

4:20–23	15:28
6:12	16:2
6:14	16:23
6:18	

Listen

15:31	19:20
18:13	21:28
18:15	

Think before You Speak

12:18	21:23
14:29	26:4
15:28	29:20
16:32	

Timing

15:23	
25:11	

Don't Talk Too Much

10:19	18:2
11:12–13	20:19
13:3	21:23
17:27–28	

Avoid Nagging

17:9
21:9

Use a Calm, Soft Answer

15:1	16:1
15:4	25:15

Ignore Results

12:16
19:11

Speak the Truth

12:17	26:18–19, 22
12:22	28:23
16:13	29:5
19:5	

Avoid Quarrels

17:14	26:21
20:3	

SUGGESTIONS FOR QUIET TIME

Make your own Quiet Time notebook. Study several verses each day and write the answers to these questions:

1. What does this verse say?
2. What does this verse say to me?
3. What is my response to this verse?

EXAMPLE: Topic—The Power of Our Words
June 15
Proverbs 25:11—"Like apples of gold in settings of silver is a word spoken in right circumstances."

Q. 1. *What does this verse say?*
It is very pleasant and wonderful to have the right thing to say at the right time.
Q. 2. *What does this verse say to me?*
I can be an encouragement and help to those around me when I say the right things at the right times.
Q. 3. *What is my response to this verse?*
"Lord, please help me today to watch what I say to my husband and children. Give me the right words at the right time! Help me realize the importance of timing."

Hide God's Word in Your Heart

The psalmist says, "Thy word have I hid in mine heart, that I might not sin against thee" (Ps. 119:11, KJV). God says we become what we think about, what we dwell on, and what we hide in our hearts. We have really found this to be true! When we think negatively, we become negative people. Why not try storing some new verses in your brain this summer? We have already looked at how practical it is to know Colossians 3:12–15.

Let's try applying another verse. In Ephesians 4:29 we read: "Let no unwholesome word proceed from your mouth, but only such a word as is good for edification according to the need of the moment, that it may give grace to those who hear." If you have memorized this, what will happen the next time you say something negative to your child? Probably this verse will cause you to gulp and rephrase your negative statement! Hiding God's Word in our hearts helps us see God's perspective instead of our muddled one.

Why not memorize one verse for each subtopic of the communication Bible study this summer? Choose your own or use the following.

1. *The Power of Our Words*

"Death and life are in the power of the tongue" (Prov. 18:21).

2. *The Source of Our Words*

"The heart of the righteous ponders how to answer, but the mouth of the wicked pours out evil things" (Prov. 15:28).

3. *Listen!*

"He who gives an answer before he hears, it is folly and shame to him" (Prov. 18:13).

4. *Think before You Speak!*

"He who is slow to anger is better than the mighty, and he who rules his spirit, than he who captures a city" (Prov. 16:32).

5. *Timing*

"A man has joy in an apt answer, and how delightful is a timely word!" (Prov. 15:23).

6. *Don't Talk Too Much*

"The one who guards his mouth preserves his life; the one who opens wide his lips comes to ruin" (Prov. 13:3).

7. *Avoid Nagging*

"It is better to live in a corner of a roof, than in a house shared with a contentious woman" (Prov. 21:9).

8. *Use a Calm, Soft Answer*

"A gentle answer turns away wrath, but a harsh word stirs up anger" (Prov. 15:1).

9. *Ignore Insults*

"A man's discretion makes him slow to anger, and it is his glory to overlook a transgression" (Prov. 19:11).

10. *Speak the Truth*

"A false witness will not go unpunished, and he who tells lies will not escape" (Prov. 19:5).

11. *Avoid Quarrels*

"Keeping away from strife is an honor for a man, but any fool will quarrel" (Prov. 20:3).

TIPS FOR HIDING THE WORD

1. Write verses out on index cards. Keep a card above the sink; doing the dishes does not require all of our brainpower!

2. Review daily—take five or ten minutes to go over verses.

3. When memorizing, write verses several times until you can say them.

4. Meditate on verses and look for ways to apply them daily.

5. Share with one other person the verses you are learning.

6. Reap benefits as you relate and communicate with others!

Notes

Chapter 1
1. Author unknown, from Evelyn and J. Allen Petersen, *For Women Only* (Wheaton, IL: Tyndale, 1975).

Chapter 2
1. Stephen Douglass, *Managing Yourself* (San Bernardino, CA: Here's Life Publishers, 1978), 1.

Chapter 4
1. Dr. Ross Campbell, *How to Really Love Your Child* (Wheaton, IL: Victor Books, 1978), 55.
2. Linda Dillow, *Priority Planner* (Nashville, TN: Thomas Nelson, 1977).
3. Helen Young, "It's Not Long from Two to Ten," *Family Life Today*, July 1977.

Chapter 5
1. H. Norman Wright, *Communication and Conflict Resolution in Marriage* (Elgin, IL: David C. Cook, 1977), 6.
2. H. Norman Wright, *Communication: Key to Your Marriage* (Glendale, CA: Regal, 1974), 55.
3. Dr. Haim Ginott, *Between Parent and Child* (New York: Avon, 1965), 25.

Chapter 6
1. *Family Life Today*, Sept. 1979, adapted from 23, 24.

Chapter 7
1. "Fabulous Freebies," *Family Circle*, 28 Aug. 1979, 53.

Chapter 8
1. We thank Gail Seidel for allowing us to reproduce her Super Summer Schedule.

Chapter 9
1. Wayne Rickerson, *Good Time for Your Family* (Glendale, CA: Regal, 1976), 20.

Chapter 10
1. "Retirement Home," *Family Life Today*, Sept. 1978, 29.

Chapter 11
1. Editorial page, *Family Life Today*, July 1975, 3.

Chapter 12
1. Charlie Shedd, *You Can Be a Great Parent* (Waco, TX: Word Books, 1970), 63.
2. Ibid., 67.

Chapter 14
1. Thanks to Sherri Gardner Howell and the *Knoxville News-Sentinel* for allowing us to use her helpful suggestions for working parents.
2. Thanks to Ina Hughs and the *Knoxville News-Sentinel* for allowing us to use excerpts from "Ode to Working Mothers" by Ina Hughs, *News-Sentinel* staff writer, *The Knoxville News-Sentinel*, 13 May 1990, 1.
3. Dave and Claudia Arp, *60 One-Minute Family Builders* (Brentwood, TN: Wolgemuth & Hyatt), 16.

Chapter 17
1. Gail Denham, "A Roots Book," *Family Life Today*, Jan. 1978.
2. James Dobson, "Traditions," *Family Life Today*, Dec. 1979.
3. Adapted from a poem by Bill Clark.

Appendix II
1. The Proverbs study is taken from H. Norman Wright, *Communication and Conflict Resolution in Marriage* (Elgin, IL: David C. Cook, 1977), 4.

Index of
Children's Day Ideas

	page
1. Pool Picnic	25
2. A Day at the Museum	26
3. Creative Collage	28
4. Slide Show	29
5. Send a Story to Friends	30
6. Let's Crochet	33
7. Creative Cooking	34
8. Backyard Circus	38
9. A Trip to the Zoo	42
10. Creative Clay Day	43
11. Finger Painting	45
12. Making Puppets	63
13. "Inner Beauty" Discussion Time	70

	page
14. Special Person Party	75
15. Letter-Writing Day	80
16. Send for Summertime Freebies	81
17. Plants Grow and So Do I	101
18. "Sonshine Children's Day" (Scripture memory)	103
19. Visit a Nursing or Retirement Home	111
20. Making Cards to Send	112
21. Send a Cookie Gift	113
22. Send a Missionary Box	114
23. Make a Travel Notebook	117

About the Authors

"Parenting can be fun!" say Claudia Arp and Linda Dillow. And they have the years of experience to prove it. Claudia is the mother of three sons and two daughters-in-law, and Linda, the mother of two daughters and two sons.

When Claudia and Linda first met in the 1970s, they were living with their husbands, Dave and Jody, in Vienna, Austria. The two women discovered they had a mutual love for marriage, family, and creative fun and began to travel together throughout Europe, leading marriage and family seminars. On a train trip through Germany, the idea for *Sanity in the Summertime* was born. After two years of research, including home-testing creative ideas on the Dillow and Arp children and weekly meetings, *Sanity* was published.

Claudia and Dave returned to the United States and settled in Knoxville, Tennessee, in 1982. Since then, Claudia has written a book on parenting adolescents, *Almost 13,* and has founded MOM's Support Groups throughout the country to help parents build positive relationships with their children. She and Dave cofounded Marriage Alive International, Inc., a ministry for family life education. And together, they have authored six books on marriage and family enrichment, including *Ten Dates for Mates*. They also have a daily radio program called "The Family Workshop."

Linda continues to live with husband Jody in Vienna, Austria. Author of *Creative Counterpart* and *Priority Planner,* Linda works with her husband to train Christian leaders throughout Europe.

Resources Available from Marriage Alive

Building Positive Relationships with Children

MOM's Support Group is a proven, family enrichment resource that is providing moms with supportive friendships and helping them build positive relationships with their children. MOM's is being used by churches and small groups across the United States and in Europe to help moms enjoy motherhood while they live through it!

Endorsed by:
- *Josh McDowell*
- *David & Vera Mace*
- *Stephen Brown*
- *Dr. D. James Kennedy*
- *Vonette Bright*
- *Jeanne Hendricks*
- *Dr. Howard Hendricks*

Package includes:
Leader's Guide
Study Books
Videos

Building Positive Relationships for the Adolescent Years

This versatile program includes a five-part video series, a Leader's Guide and Parent's individual study book.

Endorsed by:
- *Jeb Bush* •*Rosey Grier*
- *Don Schula*
- *Edward James Olmos*
- *Informed Families of Dade County, Florida*
- *Family Foundation of Savannah*

Mom's & Dad's Support Group is being used by schools, churches and groups across the country, to help parents relate to other parents and offers practical guidance in preparing for and surviving the adolescent years.

For More Information write:
Marriage Alive International, Inc.
P.O. Box 90303, Knoxville, TN 37990
or call (615) 691-MOMS or 691-8505